SCRIPTURE
JOURNAL

ENGLISH STANDARD VERSION

MATTHEW

CROSSWAY

WHEATON, ILLINOIS — ESV.ORG

ESV® Scripture Journal: Matthew

The Holy Bible, English Standard Version® (ESV®)
Copyright © 2001 by Crossway,
a publishing ministry of Good News Publishers.
All rights reserved.

ESV® Text Edition: 2016

Printed in China
Published by Crossway
Wheaton, Illinois 60187, U.S.A.
crossway.org

Crossway is a not-for-profit publishing ministry that exists solely for the purpose of publishing the Good News of the Gospel and the Truth of God's Word, the Bible. A portion of the purchase price of every ESV Bible is donated to help support Bible distribution ministry around the world.

The ESV Bible is free online and on mobile devices everywhere worldwide, including a selection of free Bible resources, at esv.org.

RRDS	26	25	24	23	22	21	20	19	18	17
12	11	10	9	8	7	6	5	4	3	2	1

PREFACE

The Bible

The words of the Bible are the very words of God our Creator speaking to us. They are completely truthful;[1] they are pure;[2] they are powerful;[3] and they are wise and righteous.[4] We should read these words with reverence and awe,[5] and with joy and delight.[6] Through these words God gives us eternal life,[7] and daily nourishes our spiritual lives.[8]

The ESV Translation

The English Standard Version® (ESV®) stands in the classic stream of English Bible translations that goes back nearly five centuries. In this stream, accurate faithfulness to the original text is combined with simplicity, beauty, and dignity of expression. Our goal has been to carry forward this legacy for this generation and generations to come.

The ESV is an "essentially literal" translation that seeks as far as possible to reproduce the meaning and structure of the original text and the personal style of each Bible writer. We have sought to be "as literal as possible" while maintaining clear expression and literary excellence. Therefore the ESV is well suited for both personal reading and church ministry, for devotional reflection and serious study, and for Scripture memorization.

---

[1] Ps. 119:160; Prov. 30:5; Titus 1:2; Heb. 6:18 [2] Ps. 12:6 [3] Jer. 23:29; Heb. 4:12; 1 Pet. 1:23
[4] Ps. 19:7–11 [5] Deut. 28:58; Ps. 119:74; Isa. 66:2 [6] Ps. 19:7–11; 119:14, 97, 103; Jer. 15:16
[7] John 6:68; 1 Pet. 1:23 [8] Deut. 32:46; Matt. 4:4

The ESV Publishing Team

The ESV publishing team has included more than a hundred people. The fourteen-member Translation Oversight Committee benefited from the work of fifty biblical experts serving as Translation Review Scholars and from the comments of the more than fifty members of the Advisory Council. This international team from many denominations shares a common commitment to the truth of God's Word and to historic Christian orthodoxy.

To God's Honor and Praise

We know that no Bible translation is perfect; but we also know that God uses imperfect and inadequate things to his honor and praise. So to God the Father, Son, and Holy Spirit—and to his people—we offer what we have done, with our prayers that it may prove useful, with gratitude for much help given, and with ongoing wonder that our God should ever have entrusted to us so momentous a task.

To God alone be the glory!
The Translation Oversight Committee

MATTHEW

The Genealogy of Jesus Christ

1 The book of the genealogy of Jesus Christ, the son of David, the son of Abraham.

² Abraham was the father of Isaac, and Isaac the father of Jacob, and Jacob the father of Judah and his brothers, ³ and Judah the father of Perez and Zerah by Tamar, and Perez the father of Hezron, and Hezron the father of Ram, ⁴ and Ram the father of Amminadab, and Amminadab the father of Nahshon, and Nahshon the father of Salmon, ⁵ and Salmon the father of Boaz by Rahab, and Boaz the father of Obed by Ruth, and Obed the father of Jesse, ⁶ and Jesse the father of David the king.

And David was the father of Solomon by the wife of Uriah, ⁷ and Solomon the father of Rehoboam, and Rehoboam the father of Abijah, and Abijah the father of Asaph, ⁸ and Asaph the father of Jehoshaphat, and Jehoshaphat the father of Joram, and Joram the father of Uzziah, ⁹ and Uzziah the father of Jotham, and Jotham the father of Ahaz, and Ahaz the father of Hezekiah, ¹⁰ and Hezekiah the father of Manasseh, and Manasseh the father of Amos, and Amos the father of Josiah, ¹¹ and Josiah the father of Jechoniah and his brothers, at the time of the deportation to Babylon.

¹² And after the deportation to Babylon: Jechoniah was the father of Shealtiel, and Shealtiel the father of Zerubbabel, ¹³ and Zerubbabel the father of Abiud, and Abiud the father of Eliakim, and Eliakim the father of Azor, ¹⁴ and Azor the father of Zadok, and Zadok the father of Achim, and Achim the father of Eliud, ¹⁵ and Eliud the father of Eleazar, and Eleazar the father of Matthan, and Matthan the father of Jacob, ¹⁶ and Jacob the father of Joseph the husband of Mary, of whom Jesus was born, who is called Christ.

¹⁷ So all the generations from Abraham to David were fourteen generations, and from David to the deportation to Babylon fourteen generations, and from the deportation to Babylon to the Christ fourteen generations.

The Birth of Jesus Christ

¹⁸ Now the birth of Jesus Christ took place in this way. When his mother Mary had been betrothed to Joseph, before they came together she was found to be with child from the Holy Spirit. ¹⁹ And her husband Joseph, being a just man and unwilling to put her to shame, resolved to divorce her quietly. ²⁰ But as he considered these things, behold, an angel of the Lord appeared to him in a dream, saying, "Joseph, son of David, do not fear to take Mary as your wife, for that which is conceived in her is from the Holy Spirit. ²¹ She will bear a son, and you shall call his name Jesus, for he will save his people from their sins." ²² All this took place to fulfill what the Lord had spoken by the prophet:

23   "Behold, the virgin shall conceive and bear a son,
            and they shall call his name Immanuel"

(which means, God with us). ²⁴ When Joseph woke from sleep, he did as the angel of the Lord commanded him: he took his wife, ²⁵ but knew her not until she had given birth to a son. And he called his name Jesus.

The Visit of the Wise Men

2 Now after Jesus was born in Bethlehem of Judea in the days of Herod the king, behold, wise men from the east came to Jerusalem, ² saying, "Where is he who has been born king of the Jews? For we saw his star when it rose and have come to worship him." ³ When Herod the king heard this, he was troubled, and all Jerusalem with him; ⁴ and assembling all the chief priests and scribes of the people, he inquired of them where the Christ was to be born. ⁵ They told him, "In Bethlehem of Judea, for so it is written by the prophet:

6   " 'And you, O Bethlehem, in the land of Judah,
            are by no means least among the rulers of Judah;
        for from you shall come a ruler
            who will shepherd my people Israel.' "

⁷ Then Herod summoned the wise men secretly and ascertained from them what time the star had appeared. ⁸ And he sent them to Bethlehem, saying, "Go and search diligently for the child, and when you have found him, bring me word, that I too may come and worship him." ⁹ After listening to the king, they went on their way. And behold, the star that they had seen when it rose went before them until it came to rest over the place where the child was. ¹⁰ When they saw the star, they rejoiced exceedingly with great joy. ¹¹ And going into the

house, they saw the child with Mary his mother, and they fell down and worshiped him. Then, opening their treasures, they offered him gifts, gold and frankincense and myrrh. [12] And being warned in a dream not to return to Herod, they departed to their own country by another way.

The Flight to Egypt

[13] Now when they had departed, behold, an angel of the Lord appeared to Joseph in a dream and said, "Rise, take the child and his mother, and flee to Egypt, and remain there until I tell you, for Herod is about to search for the child, to destroy him." [14] And he rose and took the child and his mother by night and departed to Egypt [15] and remained there until the death of Herod. This was to fulfill what the Lord had spoken by the prophet, "Out of Egypt I called my son."

Herod Kills the Children

[16] Then Herod, when he saw that he had been tricked by the wise men, became furious, and he sent and killed all the male children in Bethlehem and in all that region who were two years old or under, according to the time that he had ascertained from the wise men. [17] Then was fulfilled what was spoken by the prophet Jeremiah:

[18]   "A voice was heard in Ramah,
              weeping and loud lamentation,
          Rachel weeping for her children;
              she refused to be comforted, because they are no
                  more."

The Return to Nazareth

19 But when Herod died, behold, an angel of the Lord appeared in a dream to Joseph in Egypt, **20** saying, "Rise, take the child and his mother and go to the land of Israel, for those who sought the child's life are dead." **21** And he rose and took the child and his mother and went to the land of Israel. **22** But when he heard that Archelaus was reigning over Judea in place of his father Herod, he was afraid to go there, and being warned in a dream he withdrew to the district of Galilee. **23** And he went and lived in a city called Nazareth, so that what was spoken by the prophets might be fulfilled, that he would be called a Nazarene.

John the Baptist Prepares the Way

3 In those days John the Baptist came preaching in the wilderness of Judea, **2** "Repent, for the kingdom of heaven is at hand." **3** For this is he who was spoken of by the prophet Isaiah when he said,

> "The voice of one crying in the wilderness:
> 'Prepare the way of the Lord;
>   make his paths straight.'"

4 Now John wore a garment of camel's hair and a leather belt around his waist, and his food was locusts and wild honey. **5** Then Jerusalem and all Judea and all the region about the Jordan were going out to him, **6** and they were baptized by him in the river Jordan, confessing their sins.

7 But when he saw many of the Pharisees and Sadducees coming to his baptism, he said to them, "You brood of vipers!

Who warned you to flee from the wrath to come? [8] Bear fruit in keeping with repentance. [9] And do not presume to say to yourselves, 'We have Abraham as our father,' for I tell you, God is able from these stones to raise up children for Abraham. [10] Even now the axe is laid to the root of the trees. Every tree therefore that does not bear good fruit is cut down and thrown into the fire.

[11] "I baptize you with water for repentance, but he who is coming after me is mightier than I, whose sandals I am not worthy to carry. He will baptize you with the Holy Spirit and fire. [12] His winnowing fork is in his hand, and he will clear his threshing floor and gather his wheat into the barn, but the chaff he will burn with unquenchable fire."

The Baptism of Jesus

[13] Then Jesus came from Galilee to the Jordan to John, to be baptized by him. [14] John would have prevented him, saying, "I need to be baptized by you, and do you come to me?" [15] But Jesus answered him, "Let it be so now, for thus it is fitting for us to fulfill all righteousness." Then he consented. [16] And when Jesus was baptized, immediately he went up from the water, and behold, the heavens were opened to him, and he saw the Spirit of God descending like a dove and coming to rest on him; [17] and behold, a voice from heaven said, "This is my beloved Son, with whom I am well pleased."

The Temptation of Jesus

4 Then Jesus was led up by the Spirit into the wilderness to be tempted by the devil. [2] And after fasting forty days and forty nights, he was hungry. [3] And the tempter came and said

to him, "If you are the Son of God, command these stones to become loaves of bread." [4] But he answered, "It is written,

> "'Man shall not live by bread alone,
>   but by every word that comes from the mouth of
>   God.'"

[5] Then the devil took him to the holy city and set him on the pinnacle of the temple [6] and said to him, "If you are the Son of God, throw yourself down, for it is written,

> "'He will command his angels concerning you,'

and

> "'On their hands they will bear you up,
>   lest you strike your foot against a stone.'"

[7] Jesus said to him, "Again it is written, 'You shall not put the Lord your God to the test.'" [8] Again, the devil took him to a very high mountain and showed him all the kingdoms of the world and their glory. [9] And he said to him, "All these I will give you, if you will fall down and worship me." [10] Then Jesus said to him, "Be gone, Satan! For it is written,

> "'You shall worship the Lord your God
>   and him only shall you serve.'"

[11] Then the devil left him, and behold, angels came and were ministering to him.

Jesus Begins His Ministry

¹² Now when he heard that John had been arrested, he withdrew into Galilee. ¹³ And leaving Nazareth he went and lived in Capernaum by the sea, in the territory of Zebulun and Naphtali, ¹⁴ so that what was spoken by the prophet Isaiah might be fulfilled:

¹⁵   "The land of Zebulun and the land of Naphtali,
        the way of the sea, beyond the Jordan, Galilee of
            the Gentiles—
¹⁶   the people dwelling in darkness
        have seen a great light,
    and for those dwelling in the region and shadow of
            death,
        on them a light has dawned."

¹⁷ From that time Jesus began to preach, saying, "Repent, for the kingdom of heaven is at hand."

Jesus Calls the First Disciples

¹⁸ While walking by the Sea of Galilee, he saw two brothers, Simon (who is called Peter) and Andrew his brother, casting a net into the sea, for they were fishermen. ¹⁹ And he said to them, "Follow me, and I will make you fishers of men." ²⁰ Immediately they left their nets and followed him. ²¹ And going on from there he saw two other brothers, James the son of Zebedee and John his brother, in the boat with Zebedee their father, mending their nets, and he called them. ²² Immediately they left the boat and their father and followed him.

Jesus Ministers to Great Crowds

²³ And he went throughout all Galilee, teaching in their synagogues and proclaiming the gospel of the kingdom and healing every disease and every affliction among the people. ²⁴ So his fame spread throughout all Syria, and they brought him all the sick, those afflicted with various diseases and pains, those oppressed by demons, those having seizures, and paralytics, and he healed them. ²⁵ And great crowds followed him from Galilee and the Decapolis, and from Jerusalem and Judea, and from beyond the Jordan.

The Sermon on the Mount

5 Seeing the crowds, he went up on the mountain, and when he sat down, his disciples came to him.

The Beatitudes

² And he opened his mouth and taught them, saying:

³ "Blessed are the poor in spirit, for theirs is the kingdom of heaven.

⁴ "Blessed are those who mourn, for they shall be comforted.

⁵ "Blessed are the meek, for they shall inherit the earth.

⁶ "Blessed are those who hunger and thirst for righteousness, for they shall be satisfied.

⁷ "Blessed are the merciful, for they shall receive mercy.

⁸ "Blessed are the pure in heart, for they shall see God.

⁹ "Blessed are the peacemakers, for they shall be called sons of God.

¹⁰ "Blessed are those who are persecuted for righteousness' sake, for theirs is the kingdom of heaven.

¹¹ "Blessed are you when others revile you and persecute

you and utter all kinds of evil against you falsely on my account. [12] Rejoice and be glad, for your reward is great in heaven, for so they persecuted the prophets who were before you.

Salt and Light

[13] "You are the salt of the earth, but if salt has lost its taste, how shall its saltiness be restored? It is no longer good for anything except to be thrown out and trampled under people's feet. [14] "You are the light of the world. A city set on a hill cannot be hidden. [15] Nor do people light a lamp and put it under a basket, but on a stand, and it gives light to all in the house. [16] In the same way, let your light shine before others, so that they may see your good works and give glory to your Father who is in heaven.

Christ Came to Fulfill the Law

[17] "Do not think that I have come to abolish the Law or the Prophets; I have not come to abolish them but to fulfill them. [18] For truly, I say to you, until heaven and earth pass away, not an iota, not a dot, will pass from the Law until all is accomplished. [19] Therefore whoever relaxes one of the least of these commandments and teaches others to do the same will be called least in the kingdom of heaven, but whoever does them and teaches them will be called great in the kingdom of heaven. [20] For I tell you, unless your righteousness exceeds that of the scribes and Pharisees, you will never enter the kingdom of heaven.

Anger

[21] "You have heard that it was said to those of old, 'You shall not murder; and whoever murders will be liable to judgment.'

²² But I say to you that everyone who is angry with his brother will be liable to judgment; whoever insults his brother will be liable to the council; and whoever says, 'You fool!' will be liable to the hell of fire. ²³ So if you are offering your gift at the altar and there remember that your brother has something against you, ²⁴ leave your gift there before the altar and go. First be reconciled to your brother, and then come and offer your gift. ²⁵ Come to terms quickly with your accuser while you are going with him to court, lest your accuser hand you over to the judge, and the judge to the guard, and you be put in prison. ²⁶ Truly, I say to you, you will never get out until you have paid the last penny.

Lust

²⁷ "You have heard that it was said, 'You shall not commit adultery.' ²⁸ But I say to you that everyone who looks at a woman with lustful intent has already committed adultery with her in his heart. ²⁹ If your right eye causes you to sin, tear it out and throw it away. For it is better that you lose one of your members than that your whole body be thrown into hell. ³⁰ And if your right hand causes you to sin, cut it off and throw it away. For it is better that you lose one of your members than that your whole body go into hell.

Divorce

³¹ "It was also said, 'Whoever divorces his wife, let him give her a certificate of divorce.' ³² But I say to you that everyone who divorces his wife, except on the ground of sexual immorality, makes her commit adultery, and whoever marries a divorced woman commits adultery.

Oaths

33 "Again you have heard that it was said to those of old, 'You shall not swear falsely, but shall perform to the Lord what you have sworn.' **34** But I say to you, Do not take an oath at all, either by heaven, for it is the throne of God, **35** or by the earth, for it is his footstool, or by Jerusalem, for it is the city of the great King. **36** And do not take an oath by your head, for you cannot make one hair white or black. **37** Let what you say be simply 'Yes' or 'No'; anything more than this comes from evil.

Retaliation

38 "You have heard that it was said, 'An eye for an eye and a tooth for a tooth.' **39** But I say to you, Do not resist the one who is evil. But if anyone slaps you on the right cheek, turn to him the other also. **40** And if anyone would sue you and take your tunic, let him have your cloak as well. **41** And if anyone forces you to go one mile, go with him two miles. **42** Give to the one who begs from you, and do not refuse the one who would borrow from you.

Love Your Enemies

43 "You have heard that it was said, 'You shall love your neighbor and hate your enemy.' **44** But I say to you, Love your enemies and pray for those who persecute you, **45** so that you may be sons of your Father who is in heaven. For he makes his sun rise on the evil and on the good, and sends rain on the just and on the unjust. **46** For if you love those who love you, what reward do you have? Do not even the tax collectors do the same? **47** And if you greet only your brothers, what more are you doing than others? Do not even the Gentiles do the same? **48** You therefore must be perfect, as your heavenly Father is perfect.

Giving to the Needy

6 "Beware of practicing your righteousness before other people in order to be seen by them, for then you will have no reward from your Father who is in heaven.

² "Thus, when you give to the needy, sound no trumpet before you, as the hypocrites do in the synagogues and in the streets, that they may be praised by others. Truly, I say to you, they have received their reward. ³ But when you give to the needy, do not let your left hand know what your right hand is doing, ⁴ so that your giving may be in secret. And your Father who sees in secret will reward you.

The Lord's Prayer

⁵ "And when you pray, you must not be like the hypocrites. For they love to stand and pray in the synagogues and at the street corners, that they may be seen by others. Truly, I say to you, they have received their reward. ⁶ But when you pray, go into your room and shut the door and pray to your Father who is in secret. And your Father who sees in secret will reward you.

⁷ "And when you pray, do not heap up empty phrases as the Gentiles do, for they think that they will be heard for their many words. ⁸ Do not be like them, for your Father knows what you need before you ask him. ⁹ Pray then like this:

> "Our Father in heaven,
>   hallowed be your name.
> 10   Your kingdom come,
>   your will be done,
>   on earth as it is in heaven.
> 11   Give us this day our daily bread,

12   and forgive us our debts,
          as we also have forgiven our debtors.

13   And lead us not into temptation,
          but deliver us from evil.

[14] For if you forgive others their trespasses, your heavenly Father will also forgive you, [15] but if you do not forgive others their trespasses, neither will your Father forgive your trespasses.

Fasting

[16] "And when you fast, do not look gloomy like the hypocrites, for they disfigure their faces that their fasting may be seen by others. Truly, I say to you, they have received their reward. [17] But when you fast, anoint your head and wash your face, [18] that your fasting may not be seen by others but by your Father who is in secret. And your Father who sees in secret will reward you.

Lay Up Treasures in Heaven

[19] "Do not lay up for yourselves treasures on earth, where moth and rust destroy and where thieves break in and steal, [20] but lay up for yourselves treasures in heaven, where neither moth nor rust destroys and where thieves do not break in and steal. [21] For where your treasure is, there your heart will be also.

[22] "The eye is the lamp of the body. So, if your eye is healthy, your whole body will be full of light, [23] but if your eye is bad, your whole body will be full of darkness. If then the light in you is darkness, how great is the darkness!

[24] "No one can serve two masters, for either he will hate the one and love the other, or he will be devoted to the one and despise the other. You cannot serve God and money.

Do Not Be Anxious

[25] "Therefore I tell you, do not be anxious about your life, what you will eat or what you will drink, nor about your body, what you will put on. Is not life more than food, and the body more than clothing? [26] Look at the birds of the air: they neither sow nor reap nor gather into barns, and yet your heavenly Father feeds them. Are you not of more value than they? [27] And which of you by being anxious can add a single hour to his span of life? [28] And why are you anxious about clothing? Consider the lilies of the field, how they grow: they neither toil nor spin, [29] yet I tell you, even Solomon in all his glory was not arrayed like one of these. [30] But if God so clothes the grass of the field, which today is alive and tomorrow is thrown into the oven, will he not much more clothe you, O you of little faith? [31] Therefore do not be anxious, saying, 'What shall we eat?' or 'What shall we drink?' or 'What shall we wear?' [32] For the Gentiles seek after all these things, and your heavenly Father knows that you need them all. [33] But seek first the kingdom of God and his righteousness, and all these things will be added to you.

[34] "Therefore do not be anxious about tomorrow, for tomorrow will be anxious for itself. Sufficient for the day is its own trouble.

Judging Others

7 "Judge not, that you be not judged. [2] For with the judgment you pronounce you will be judged, and with the measure you use it will be measured to you. [3] Why do you see the speck that is in your brother's eye, but do not notice the log that is in your own eye? [4] Or how can you say to your brother, 'Let me take the speck out of your eye,' when there is the log

in your own eye? [5] You hypocrite, first take the log out of your own eye, and then you will see clearly to take the speck out of your brother's eye.

[6] "Do not give dogs what is holy, and do not throw your pearls before pigs, lest they trample them underfoot and turn to attack you.

Ask, and It Will Be Given

[7] "Ask, and it will be given to you; seek, and you will find; knock, and it will be opened to you. [8] For everyone who asks receives, and the one who seeks finds, and to the one who knocks it will be opened. [9] Or which one of you, if his son asks him for bread, will give him a stone? [10] Or if he asks for a fish, will give him a serpent? [11] If you then, who are evil, know how to give good gifts to your children, how much more will your Father who is in heaven give good things to those who ask him!

The Golden Rule

[12] "So whatever you wish that others would do to you, do also to them, for this is the Law and the Prophets.

[13] "Enter by the narrow gate. For the gate is wide and the way is easy that leads to destruction, and those who enter by it are many. [14] For the gate is narrow and the way is hard that leads to life, and those who find it are few.

A Tree and Its Fruit

[15] "Beware of false prophets, who come to you in sheep's clothing but inwardly are ravenous wolves. [16] You will recognize them by their fruits. Are grapes gathered from thornbushes, or

figs from thistles? ¹⁷ So, every healthy tree bears good fruit, but the diseased tree bears bad fruit. ¹⁸ A healthy tree cannot bear bad fruit, nor can a diseased tree bear good fruit. ¹⁹ Every tree that does not bear good fruit is cut down and thrown into the fire. ²⁰ Thus you will recognize them by their fruits.

I Never Knew You

²¹ "Not everyone who says to me, 'Lord, Lord,' will enter the kingdom of heaven, but the one who does the will of my Father who is in heaven. ²² On that day many will say to me, 'Lord, Lord, did we not prophesy in your name, and cast out demons in your name, and do many mighty works in your name?' ²³ And then will I declare to them, 'I never knew you; depart from me, you workers of lawlessness.'

Build Your House on the Rock

²⁴ "Everyone then who hears these words of mine and does them will be like a wise man who built his house on the rock. ²⁵ And the rain fell, and the floods came, and the winds blew and beat on that house, but it did not fall, because it had been founded on the rock. ²⁶ And everyone who hears these words of mine and does not do them will be like a foolish man who built his house on the sand. ²⁷ And the rain fell, and the floods came, and the winds blew and beat against that house, and it fell, and great was the fall of it."

The Authority of Jesus

²⁸ And when Jesus finished these sayings, the crowds were astonished at his teaching, ²⁹ for he was teaching them as one who had authority, and not as their scribes.

Jesus Cleanses a Leper

8 When he came down from the mountain, great crowds followed him. ² And behold, a leper came to him and knelt before him, saying, "Lord, if you will, you can make me clean." ³ And Jesus stretched out his hand and touched him, saying, "I will; be clean." And immediately his leprosy was cleansed. ⁴ And Jesus said to him, "See that you say nothing to anyone, but go, show yourself to the priest and offer the gift that Moses commanded, for a proof to them."

The Faith of a Centurion

⁵ When he had entered Capernaum, a centurion came forward to him, appealing to him, ⁶ "Lord, my servant is lying paralyzed at home, suffering terribly." ⁷ And he said to him, "I will come and heal him." ⁸ But the centurion replied, "Lord, I am not worthy to have you come under my roof, but only say the word, and my servant will be healed. ⁹ For I too am a man under authority, with soldiers under me. And I say to one, 'Go,' and he goes, and to another, 'Come,' and he comes, and to my servant, 'Do this,' and he does it." ¹⁰ When Jesus heard this, he marveled and said to those who followed him, "Truly, I tell you, with no one in Israel have I found such faith. ¹¹ I tell you, many will come from east and west and recline at table with Abraham, Isaac, and Jacob in the kingdom of heaven, ¹² while the sons of the kingdom will be thrown into the outer darkness. In that place there will be weeping and gnashing of teeth." ¹³ And to the centurion Jesus said, "Go; let it be done for you as you have believed." And the servant was healed at that very moment.

Jesus Heals Many

14 And when Jesus entered Peter's house, he saw his mother-in-law lying sick with a fever. **15** He touched her hand, and the fever left her, and she rose and began to serve him. **16** That evening they brought to him many who were oppressed by demons, and he cast out the spirits with a word and healed all who were sick. **17** This was to fulfill what was spoken by the prophet Isaiah: "He took our illnesses and bore our diseases."

The Cost of Following Jesus

18 Now when Jesus saw a crowd around him, he gave orders to go over to the other side. **19** And a scribe came up and said to him, "Teacher, I will follow you wherever you go." **20** And Jesus said to him, "Foxes have holes, and birds of the air have nests, but the Son of Man has nowhere to lay his head." **21** Another of the disciples said to him, "Lord, let me first go and bury my father." **22** And Jesus said to him, "Follow me, and leave the dead to bury their own dead."

Jesus Calms a Storm

23 And when he got into the boat, his disciples followed him. **24** And behold, there arose a great storm on the sea, so that the boat was being swamped by the waves; but he was asleep. **25** And they went and woke him, saying, "Save us, Lord; we are perishing." **26** And he said to them, "Why are you afraid, O you of little faith?" Then he rose and rebuked the winds and the sea, and there was a great calm. **27** And the men marveled, saying, "What sort of man is this, that even winds and sea obey him?"

Jesus Heals Two Men with Demons

²⁸ And when he came to the other side, to the country of the Gadarenes, two demon-possessed men met him, coming out of the tombs, so fierce that no one could pass that way. ²⁹ And behold, they cried out, "What have you to do with us, O Son of God? Have you come here to torment us before the time?" ³⁰ Now a herd of many pigs was feeding at some distance from them. ³¹ And the demons begged him, saying, "If you cast us out, send us away into the herd of pigs." ³² And he said to them, "Go." So they came out and went into the pigs, and behold, the whole herd rushed down the steep bank into the sea and drowned in the waters. ³³ The herdsmen fled, and going into the city they told everything, especially what had happened to the demon-possessed men. ³⁴ And behold, all the city came out to meet Jesus, and when they saw him, they begged him to leave their region.

Jesus Heals a Paralytic

9 And getting into a boat he crossed over and came to his own city. ² And behold, some people brought to him a paralytic, lying on a bed. And when Jesus saw their faith, he said to the paralytic, "Take heart, my son; your sins are forgiven." ³ And behold, some of the scribes said to themselves, "This man is blaspheming." ⁴ But Jesus, knowing their thoughts, said, "Why do you think evil in your hearts? ⁵ For which is easier, to say, 'Your sins are forgiven,' or to say, 'Rise and walk'? ⁶ But that you may know that the Son of Man has authority on earth to forgive sins"—he then said to the paralytic—"Rise, pick up your bed and go home." ⁷ And he rose and went home. ⁸ When the crowds saw it, they were afraid, and they glorified God, who had given such authority to men.

Jesus Calls Matthew

⁹As Jesus passed on from there, he saw a man called Matthew sitting at the tax booth, and he said to him, "Follow me." And he rose and followed him.

¹⁰And as Jesus reclined at table in the house, behold, many tax collectors and sinners came and were reclining with Jesus and his disciples. ¹¹And when the Pharisees saw this, they said to his disciples, "Why does your teacher eat with tax collectors and sinners?" ¹²But when he heard it, he said, "Those who are well have no need of a physician, but those who are sick. ¹³Go and learn what this means: 'I desire mercy, and not sacrifice.' For I came not to call the righteous, but sinners."

A Question About Fasting

¹⁴Then the disciples of John came to him, saying, "Why do we and the Pharisees fast, but your disciples do not fast?" ¹⁵And Jesus said to them, "Can the wedding guests mourn as long as the bridegroom is with them? The days will come when the bridegroom is taken away from them, and then they will fast. ¹⁶No one puts a piece of unshrunk cloth on an old garment, for the patch tears away from the garment, and a worse tear is made. ¹⁷Neither is new wine put into old wineskins. If it is, the skins burst and the wine is spilled and the skins are destroyed. But new wine is put into fresh wineskins, and so both are preserved."

A Girl Restored to Life and a Woman Healed

¹⁸While he was saying these things to them, behold, a ruler came in and knelt before him, saying, "My daughter has just died, but come and lay your hand on her, and she will live." ¹⁹And Jesus rose and followed him, with his disciples. ²⁰And

behold, a woman who had suffered from a discharge of blood for twelve years came up behind him and touched the fringe of his garment, [21] for she said to herself, "If I only touch his garment, I will be made well." [22] Jesus turned, and seeing her he said, "Take heart, daughter; your faith has made you well." And instantly the woman was made well. [23] And when Jesus came to the ruler's house and saw the flute players and the crowd making a commotion, [24] he said, "Go away, for the girl is not dead but sleeping." And they laughed at him. [25] But when the crowd had been put outside, he went in and took her by the hand, and the girl arose. [26] And the report of this went through all that district.

Jesus Heals Two Blind Men

[27] And as Jesus passed on from there, two blind men followed him, crying aloud, "Have mercy on us, Son of David." [28] When he entered the house, the blind men came to him, and Jesus said to them, "Do you believe that I am able to do this?" They said to him, "Yes, Lord." [29] Then he touched their eyes, saying, "According to your faith be it done to you." [30] And their eyes were opened. And Jesus sternly warned them, "See that no one knows about it." [31] But they went away and spread his fame through all that district.

Jesus Heals a Man Unable to Speak

[32] As they were going away, behold, a demon-oppressed man who was mute was brought to him. [33] And when the demon had been cast out, the mute man spoke. And the crowds marveled, saying, "Never was anything like this seen in Israel." [34] But the Pharisees said, "He casts out demons by the prince of demons."

The Harvest Is Plentiful, the Laborers Few

35 And Jesus went throughout all the cities and villages, teaching in their synagogues and proclaiming the gospel of the kingdom and healing every disease and every affliction. **36** When he saw the crowds, he had compassion for them, because they were harassed and helpless, like sheep without a shepherd. **37** Then he said to his disciples, "The harvest is plentiful, but the laborers are few; **38** therefore pray earnestly to the Lord of the harvest to send out laborers into his harvest."

The Twelve Apostles

10 And he called to him his twelve disciples and gave them authority over unclean spirits, to cast them out, and to heal every disease and every affliction. **2** The names of the twelve apostles are these: first, Simon, who is called Peter, and Andrew his brother; James the son of Zebedee, and John his brother; **3** Philip and Bartholomew; Thomas and Matthew the tax collector; James the son of Alphaeus, and Thaddaeus; **4** Simon the Zealot, and Judas Iscariot, who betrayed him.

Jesus Sends Out the Twelve Apostles

5 These twelve Jesus sent out, instructing them, "Go nowhere among the Gentiles and enter no town of the Samaritans, **6** but go rather to the lost sheep of the house of Israel. **7** And proclaim as you go, saying, 'The kingdom of heaven is at hand.' **8** Heal the sick, raise the dead, cleanse lepers, cast out demons. You received without paying; give without pay. **9** Acquire no gold or silver or copper for your belts, **10** no bag for your journey, or two tunics or sandals or a staff, for the laborer deserves his food. **11** And whatever town or village you enter, find out who is worthy in it

and stay there until you depart. [12] As you enter the house, greet it. [13] And if the house is worthy, let your peace come upon it, but if it is not worthy, let your peace return to you. [14] And if anyone will not receive you or listen to your words, shake off the dust from your feet when you leave that house or town. [15] Truly, I say to you, it will be more bearable on the day of judgment for the land of Sodom and Gomorrah than for that town.

Persecution Will Come

[16] "Behold, I am sending you out as sheep in the midst of wolves, so be wise as serpents and innocent as doves. [17] Beware of men, for they will deliver you over to courts and flog you in their synagogues, [18] and you will be dragged before governors and kings for my sake, to bear witness before them and the Gentiles. [19] When they deliver you over, do not be anxious how you are to speak or what you are to say, for what you are to say will be given to you in that hour. [20] For it is not you who speak, but the Spirit of your Father speaking through you. [21] Brother will deliver brother over to death, and the father his child, and children will rise against parents and have them put to death, [22] and you will be hated by all for my name's sake. But the one who endures to the end will be saved. [23] When they persecute you in one town, flee to the next, for truly, I say to you, you will not have gone through all the towns of Israel before the Son of Man comes.

[24] "A disciple is not above his teacher, nor a servant above his master. [25] It is enough for the disciple to be like his teacher, and the servant like his master. If they have called the master of the house Beelzebul, how much more will they malign those of his household.

Have No Fear

²⁶ "So have no fear of them, for nothing is covered that will not be revealed, or hidden that will not be known. ²⁷ What I tell you in the dark, say in the light, and what you hear whispered, proclaim on the housetops. ²⁸ And do not fear those who kill the body but cannot kill the soul. Rather fear him who can destroy both soul and body in hell. ²⁹ Are not two sparrows sold for a penny? And not one of them will fall to the ground apart from your Father. ³⁰ But even the hairs of your head are all numbered. ³¹ Fear not, therefore; you are of more value than many sparrows. ³² So everyone who acknowledges me before men, I also will acknowledge before my Father who is in heaven, ³³ but whoever denies me before men, I also will deny before my Father who is in heaven.

Not Peace, but a Sword

³⁴ "Do not think that I have come to bring peace to the earth. I have not come to bring peace, but a sword. ³⁵ For I have come to set a man against his father, and a daughter against her mother, and a daughter-in-law against her mother-in-law. ³⁶ And a person's enemies will be those of his own household. ³⁷ Whoever loves father or mother more than me is not worthy of me, and whoever loves son or daughter more than me is not worthy of me. ³⁸ And whoever does not take his cross and follow me is not worthy of me. ³⁹ Whoever finds his life will lose it, and whoever loses his life for my sake will find it.

Rewards

⁴⁰ "Whoever receives you receives me, and whoever receives me receives him who sent me. ⁴¹ The one who receives a prophet

because he is a prophet will receive a prophet's reward, and the one who receives a righteous person because he is a righteous person will receive a righteous person's reward. [42] And whoever gives one of these little ones even a cup of cold water because he is a disciple, truly, I say to you, he will by no means lose his reward."

Messengers from John the Baptist

11 When Jesus had finished instructing his twelve disciples, he went on from there to teach and preach in their cities.

[2] Now when John heard in prison about the deeds of the Christ, he sent word by his disciples [3] and said to him, "Are you the one who is to come, or shall we look for another?" [4] And Jesus answered them, "Go and tell John what you hear and see: [5] the blind receive their sight and the lame walk, lepers are cleansed and the deaf hear, and the dead are raised up, and the poor have good news preached to them. [6] And blessed is the one who is not offended by me."

[7] As they went away, Jesus began to speak to the crowds concerning John: "What did you go out into the wilderness to see? A reed shaken by the wind? [8] What then did you go out to see? A man dressed in soft clothing? Behold, those who wear soft clothing are in kings' houses. [9] What then did you go out to see? A prophet? Yes, I tell you, and more than a prophet. [10] This is he of whom it is written,

> "'Behold, I send my messenger before your face,
>   who will prepare your way before you.'

[11] Truly, I say to you, among those born of women there has arisen no one greater than John the Baptist. Yet the one who is

least in the kingdom of heaven is greater than he. ¹² From the days of John the Baptist until now the kingdom of heaven has suffered violence, and the violent take it by force. ¹³ For all the Prophets and the Law prophesied until John, ¹⁴ and if you are willing to accept it, he is Elijah who is to come. ¹⁵ He who has ears to hear, let him hear.

¹⁶ "But to what shall I compare this generation? It is like children sitting in the marketplaces and calling to their playmates,

¹⁷   " 'We played the flute for you, and you did not dance;
          we sang a dirge, and you did not mourn.'

¹⁸ For John came neither eating nor drinking, and they say, 'He has a demon.' ¹⁹ The Son of Man came eating and drinking, and they say, 'Look at him! A glutton and a drunkard, a friend of tax collectors and sinners!' Yet wisdom is justified by her deeds."

Woe to Unrepentant Cities

²⁰ Then he began to denounce the cities where most of his mighty works had been done, because they did not repent. ²¹ "Woe to you, Chorazin! Woe to you, Bethsaida! For if the mighty works done in you had been done in Tyre and Sidon, they would have repented long ago in sackcloth and ashes. ²² But I tell you, it will be more bearable on the day of judgment for Tyre and Sidon than for you. ²³ And you, Capernaum, will you be exalted to heaven? You will be brought down to Hades. For if the mighty works done in you had been done in Sodom, it would have remained until this day. ²⁴ But I tell you that it will be more tolerable on the day of judgment for the land of Sodom than for you."

Come to Me, and I Will Give You Rest

²⁵ At that time Jesus declared, "I thank you, Father, Lord of heaven and earth, that you have hidden these things from the wise and understanding and revealed them to little children; ²⁶ yes, Father, for such was your gracious will. ²⁷ All things have been handed over to me by my Father, and no one knows the Son except the Father, and no one knows the Father except the Son and anyone to whom the Son chooses to reveal him. ²⁸ Come to me, all who labor and are heavy laden, and I will give you rest. ²⁹ Take my yoke upon you, and learn from me, for I am gentle and lowly in heart, and you will find rest for your souls. ³⁰ For my yoke is easy, and my burden is light."

Jesus Is Lord of the Sabbath

12 At that time Jesus went through the grainfields on the Sabbath. His disciples were hungry, and they began to pluck heads of grain and to eat. ² But when the Pharisees saw it, they said to him, "Look, your disciples are doing what is not lawful to do on the Sabbath." ³ He said to them, "Have you not read what David did when he was hungry, and those who were with him: ⁴ how he entered the house of God and ate the bread of the Presence, which it was not lawful for him to eat nor for those who were with him, but only for the priests? ⁵ Or have you not read in the Law how on the Sabbath the priests in the temple profane the Sabbath and are guiltless? ⁶ I tell you, something greater than the temple is here. ⁷ And if you had known what this means, 'I desire mercy, and not sacrifice,' you would not have condemned the guiltless. ⁸ For the Son of Man is lord of the Sabbath."

A Man with a Withered Hand

9 He went on from there and entered their synagogue. **10** And a man was there with a withered hand. And they asked him, "Is it lawful to heal on the Sabbath?"—so that they might accuse him. **11** He said to them, "Which one of you who has a sheep, if it falls into a pit on the Sabbath, will not take hold of it and lift it out? **12** Of how much more value is a man than a sheep! So it is lawful to do good on the Sabbath." **13** Then he said to the man, "Stretch out your hand." And the man stretched it out, and it was restored, healthy like the other. **14** But the Pharisees went out and conspired against him, how to destroy him.

God's Chosen Servant

15 Jesus, aware of this, withdrew from there. And many followed him, and he healed them all **16** and ordered them not to make him known. **17** This was to fulfill what was spoken by the prophet Isaiah:

18   "Behold, my servant whom I have chosen,
         my beloved with whom my soul is well pleased.
     I will put my Spirit upon him,
         and he will proclaim justice to the Gentiles.
19   He will not quarrel or cry aloud,
         nor will anyone hear his voice in the streets;
20   a bruised reed he will not break,
         and a smoldering wick he will not quench,
     until he brings justice to victory;
21   and in his name the Gentiles will hope."

Blasphemy Against the Holy Spirit

²² Then a demon-oppressed man who was blind and mute was brought to him, and he healed him, so that the man spoke and saw. ²³ And all the people were amazed, and said, "Can this be the Son of David?" ²⁴ But when the Pharisees heard it, they said, "It is only by Beelzebul, the prince of demons, that this man casts out demons." ²⁵ Knowing their thoughts, he said to them, "Every kingdom divided against itself is laid waste, and no city or house divided against itself will stand. ²⁶ And if Satan casts out Satan, he is divided against himself. How then will his kingdom stand? ²⁷ And if I cast out demons by Beelzebul, by whom do your sons cast them out? Therefore they will be your judges. ²⁸ But if it is by the Spirit of God that I cast out demons, then the kingdom of God has come upon you. ²⁹ Or how can someone enter a strong man's house and plunder his goods, unless he first binds the strong man? Then indeed he may plunder his house. ³⁰ Whoever is not with me is against me, and whoever does not gather with me scatters. ³¹ Therefore I tell you, every sin and blasphemy will be forgiven people, but the blasphemy against the Spirit will not be forgiven. ³² And whoever speaks a word against the Son of Man will be forgiven, but whoever speaks against the Holy Spirit will not be forgiven, either in this age or in the age to come.

A Tree Is Known by Its Fruit

³³ "Either make the tree good and its fruit good, or make the tree bad and its fruit bad, for the tree is known by its fruit. ³⁴ You brood of vipers! How can you speak good, when you are evil? For out of the abundance of the heart the mouth speaks. ³⁵ The good person out of his good treasure brings forth good,

and the evil person out of his evil treasure brings forth evil. [36] I tell you, on the day of judgment people will give account for every careless word they speak, [37] for by your words you will be justified, and by your words you will be condemned."

The Sign of Jonah

[38] Then some of the scribes and Pharisees answered him, saying, "Teacher, we wish to see a sign from you." [39] But he answered them, "An evil and adulterous generation seeks for a sign, but no sign will be given to it except the sign of the prophet Jonah. [40] For just as Jonah was three days and three nights in the belly of the great fish, so will the Son of Man be three days and three nights in the heart of the earth. [41] The men of Nineveh will rise up at the judgment with this generation and condemn it, for they repented at the preaching of Jonah, and behold, something greater than Jonah is here. [42] The queen of the South will rise up at the judgment with this generation and condemn it, for she came from the ends of the earth to hear the wisdom of Solomon, and behold, something greater than Solomon is here.

Return of an Unclean Spirit

[43] "When the unclean spirit has gone out of a person, it passes through waterless places seeking rest, but finds none. [44] Then it says, 'I will return to my house from which I came.' And when it comes, it finds the house empty, swept, and put in order. [45] Then it goes and brings with it seven other spirits more evil than itself, and they enter and dwell there, and the last state of that person is worse than the first. So also will it be with this evil generation."

Jesus' Mother and Brothers

46 While he was still speaking to the people, behold, his mother and his brothers stood outside, asking to speak to him. **48** But he replied to the man who told him, "Who is my mother, and who are my brothers?" **49** And stretching out his hand toward his disciples, he said, "Here are my mother and my brothers! **50** For whoever does the will of my Father in heaven is my brother and sister and mother."

The Parable of the Sower

13 That same day Jesus went out of the house and sat beside the sea. **2** And great crowds gathered about him, so that he got into a boat and sat down. And the whole crowd stood on the beach. **3** And he told them many things in parables, saying: "A sower went out to sow. **4** And as he sowed, some seeds fell along the path, and the birds came and devoured them. **5** Other seeds fell on rocky ground, where they did not have much soil, and immediately they sprang up, since they had no depth of soil, **6** but when the sun rose they were scorched. And since they had no root, they withered away. **7** Other seeds fell among thorns, and the thorns grew up and choked them. **8** Other seeds fell on good soil and produced grain, some a hundredfold, some sixty, some thirty. **9** He who has ears, let him hear."

The Purpose of the Parables

10 Then the disciples came and said to him, "Why do you speak to them in parables?" **11** And he answered them, "To you it has been given to know the secrets of the kingdom of heaven, but to them it has not been given. **12** For to the one who has,

more will be given, and he will have an abundance, but from the one who has not, even what he has will be taken away. ¹³ This is why I speak to them in parables, because seeing they do not see, and hearing they do not hear, nor do they understand. ¹⁴ Indeed, in their case the prophecy of Isaiah is fulfilled that says:

> " ' "You will indeed hear but never understand,
>   and you will indeed see but never perceive."
> ¹⁵   For this people's heart has grown dull,
>   and with their ears they can barely hear,
>   and their eyes they have closed,
> lest they should see with their eyes
>   and hear with their ears
> and understand with their heart
>   and turn, and I would heal them.'

¹⁶ But blessed are your eyes, for they see, and your ears, for they hear. ¹⁷ For truly, I say to you, many prophets and righteous people longed to see what you see, and did not see it, and to hear what you hear, and did not hear it.

The Parable of the Sower Explained

¹⁸ "Hear then the parable of the sower: ¹⁹ When anyone hears the word of the kingdom and does not understand it, the evil one comes and snatches away what has been sown in his heart. This is what was sown along the path. ²⁰ As for what was sown on rocky ground, this is the one who hears the word and immediately receives it with joy, ²¹ yet he has no root in himself, but endures for a while, and when tribulation or persecution

arises on account of the word, immediately he falls away. [22] As for what was sown among thorns, this is the one who hears the word, but the cares of the world and the deceitfulness of riches choke the word, and it proves unfruitful. [23] As for what was sown on good soil, this is the one who hears the word and understands it. He indeed bears fruit and yields, in one case a hundredfold, in another sixty, and in another thirty."

The Parable of the Weeds

[24] He put another parable before them, saying, "The kingdom of heaven may be compared to a man who sowed good seed in his field, [25] but while his men were sleeping, his enemy came and sowed weeds among the wheat and went away. [26] So when the plants came up and bore grain, then the weeds appeared also. [27] And the servants of the master of the house came and said to him, 'Master, did you not sow good seed in your field? How then does it have weeds?' [28] He said to them, 'An enemy has done this.' So the servants said to him, 'Then do you want us to go and gather them?' [29] But he said, 'No, lest in gathering the weeds you root up the wheat along with them. [30] Let both grow together until the harvest, and at harvest time I will tell the reapers, "Gather the weeds first and bind them in bundles to be burned, but gather the wheat into my barn."'"

The Mustard Seed and the Leaven

[31] He put another parable before them, saying, "The kingdom of heaven is like a grain of mustard seed that a man took and sowed in his field. [32] It is the smallest of all seeds, but when it has grown it is larger than all the garden plants and becomes

a tree, so that the birds of the air come and make nests in its branches."

[33] He told them another parable. "The kingdom of heaven is like leaven that a woman took and hid in three measures of flour, till it was all leavened."

Prophecy and Parables

[34] All these things Jesus said to the crowds in parables; indeed, he said nothing to them without a parable. [35] This was to fulfill what was spoken by the prophet:

> "I will open my mouth in parables;
>   I will utter what has been hidden since the
>   foundation of the world."

The Parable of the Weeds Explained

[36] Then he left the crowds and went into the house. And his disciples came to him, saying, "Explain to us the parable of the weeds of the field." [37] He answered, "The one who sows the good seed is the Son of Man. [38] The field is the world, and the good seed is the sons of the kingdom. The weeds are the sons of the evil one, [39] and the enemy who sowed them is the devil. The harvest is the end of the age, and the reapers are angels. [40] Just as the weeds are gathered and burned with fire, so will it be at the end of the age. [41] The Son of Man will send his angels, and they will gather out of his kingdom all causes of sin and all law-breakers, [42] and throw them into the fiery furnace. In that place there will be weeping and gnashing of teeth. [43] Then the righteous will shine like the sun in the kingdom of their Father. He who has ears, let him hear.

The Parable of the Hidden Treasure

44 "The kingdom of heaven is like treasure hidden in a field, which a man found and covered up. Then in his joy he goes and sells all that he has and buys that field.

The Parable of the Pearl of Great Value

45 "Again, the kingdom of heaven is like a merchant in search of fine pearls, **46** who, on finding one pearl of great value, went and sold all that he had and bought it.

The Parable of the Net

47 "Again, the kingdom of heaven is like a net that was thrown into the sea and gathered fish of every kind. **48** When it was full, men drew it ashore and sat down and sorted the good into containers but threw away the bad. **49** So it will be at the end of the age. The angels will come out and separate the evil from the righteous **50** and throw them into the fiery furnace. In that place there will be weeping and gnashing of teeth.

New and Old Treasures

51 "Have you understood all these things?" They said to him, "Yes." **52** And he said to them, "Therefore every scribe who has been trained for the kingdom of heaven is like a master of a house, who brings out of his treasure what is new and what is old."

Jesus Rejected at Nazareth

53 And when Jesus had finished these parables, he went away from there, **54** and coming to his hometown he taught them in their synagogue, so that they were astonished, and

said, "Where did this man get this wisdom and these mighty works? ⁵⁵ Is not this the carpenter's son? Is not his mother called Mary? And are not his brothers James and Joseph and Simon and Judas? ⁵⁶ And are not all his sisters with us? Where then did this man get all these things?" ⁵⁷ And they took offense at him. But Jesus said to them, "A prophet is not without honor except in his hometown and in his own household." ⁵⁸ And he did not do many mighty works there, because of their unbelief.

The Death of John the Baptist

14 At that time Herod the tetrarch heard about the fame of Jesus, ² and he said to his servants, "This is John the Baptist. He has been raised from the dead; that is why these miraculous powers are at work in him." ³ For Herod had seized John and bound him and put him in prison for the sake of Herodias, his brother Philip's wife, ⁴ because John had been saying to him, "It is not lawful for you to have her." ⁵ And though he wanted to put him to death, he feared the people, because they held him to be a prophet. ⁶ But when Herod's birthday came, the daughter of Herodias danced before the company and pleased Herod, ⁷ so that he promised with an oath to give her whatever she might ask. ⁸ Prompted by her mother, she said, "Give me the head of John the Baptist here on a platter." ⁹ And the king was sorry, but because of his oaths and his guests he commanded it to be given. ¹⁰ He sent and had John beheaded in the prison, ¹¹ and his head was brought on a platter and given to the girl, and she brought it to her mother. ¹² And his disciples came and took the body and buried it, and they went and told Jesus.

Jesus Feeds the Five Thousand

¹³ Now when Jesus heard this, he withdrew from there in a boat to a desolate place by himself. But when the crowds heard it, they followed him on foot from the towns. ¹⁴ When he went ashore he saw a great crowd, and he had compassion on them and healed their sick. ¹⁵ Now when it was evening, the disciples came to him and said, "This is a desolate place, and the day is now over; send the crowds away to go into the villages and buy food for themselves." ¹⁶ But Jesus said, "They need not go away; you give them something to eat." ¹⁷ They said to him, "We have only five loaves here and two fish." ¹⁸ And he said, "Bring them here to me." ¹⁹ Then he ordered the crowds to sit down on the grass, and taking the five loaves and the two fish, he looked up to heaven and said a blessing. Then he broke the loaves and gave them to the disciples, and the disciples gave them to the crowds. ²⁰ And they all ate and were satisfied. And they took up twelve baskets full of the broken pieces left over. ²¹ And those who ate were about five thousand men, besides women and children.

Jesus Walks on the Water

²² Immediately he made the disciples get into the boat and go before him to the other side, while he dismissed the crowds. ²³ And after he had dismissed the crowds, he went up on the mountain by himself to pray. When evening came, he was there alone, ²⁴ but the boat by this time was a long way from the land, beaten by the waves, for the wind was against them. ²⁵ And in the fourth watch of the night he came to them, walking on the sea. ²⁶ But when the disciples saw him walking on the sea, they were terrified, and said, "It is a ghost!" and they cried out in

fear. **27** But immediately Jesus spoke to them, saying, "Take heart; it is I. Do not be afraid."

28 And Peter answered him, "Lord, if it is you, command me to come to you on the water." **29** He said, "Come." So Peter got out of the boat and walked on the water and came to Jesus. **30** But when he saw the wind, he was afraid, and beginning to sink he cried out, "Lord, save me." **31** Jesus immediately reached out his hand and took hold of him, saying to him, "O you of little faith, why did you doubt?" **32** And when they got into the boat, the wind ceased. **33** And those in the boat worshiped him, saying, "Truly you are the Son of God."

Jesus Heals the Sick in Gennesaret

34 And when they had crossed over, they came to land at Gennesaret. **35** And when the men of that place recognized him, they sent around to all that region and brought to him all who were sick **36** and implored him that they might only touch the fringe of his garment. And as many as touched it were made well.

Traditions and Commandments

15 Then Pharisees and scribes came to Jesus from Jerusalem and said, **2** "Why do your disciples break the tradition of the elders? For they do not wash their hands when they eat." **3** He answered them, "And why do you break the commandment of God for the sake of your tradition? **4** For God commanded, 'Honor your father and your mother,' and, 'Whoever reviles father or mother must surely die.' **5** But you say, 'If anyone tells his father or his mother, "What you would have gained from me is given to God," **6** he need not honor his father.' So for

the sake of your tradition you have made void the word of God. ⁷You hypocrites! Well did Isaiah prophesy of you, when he said:

8   "'This people honors me with their lips,
            but their heart is far from me;
9   in vain do they worship me,
            teaching as doctrines the commandments of
            men.'"

What Defiles a Person

¹⁰And he called the people to him and said to them, "Hear and understand: ¹¹ it is not what goes into the mouth that defiles a person, but what comes out of the mouth; this defiles a person." ¹²Then the disciples came and said to him, "Do you know that the Pharisees were offended when they heard this saying?" ¹³He answered, "Every plant that my heavenly Father has not planted will be rooted up. ¹⁴Let them alone; they are blind guides. And if the blind lead the blind, both will fall into a pit." ¹⁵But Peter said to him, "Explain the parable to us." ¹⁶And he said, "Are you also still without understanding? ¹⁷Do you not see that whatever goes into the mouth passes into the stomach and is expelled? ¹⁸But what comes out of the mouth proceeds from the heart, and this defiles a person. ¹⁹For out of the heart come evil thoughts, murder, adultery, sexual immorality, theft, false witness, slander. ²⁰These are what defile a person. But to eat with unwashed hands does not defile anyone."

The Faith of a Canaanite Woman

²¹ And Jesus went away from there and withdrew to the district of Tyre and Sidon. ²²And behold, a Canaanite woman

from that region came out and was crying, "Have mercy on me, O Lord, Son of David; my daughter is severely oppressed by a demon." ²³ But he did not answer her a word. And his disciples came and begged him, saying, "Send her away, for she is crying out after us." ²⁴ He answered, "I was sent only to the lost sheep of the house of Israel." ²⁵ But she came and knelt before him, saying, "Lord, help me." ²⁶ And he answered, "It is not right to take the children's bread and throw it to the dogs." ²⁷ She said, "Yes, Lord, yet even the dogs eat the crumbs that fall from their masters' table." ²⁸ Then Jesus answered her, "O woman, great is your faith! Be it done for you as you desire." And her daughter was healed instantly.

Jesus Heals Many

²⁹ Jesus went on from there and walked beside the Sea of Galilee. And he went up on the mountain and sat down there. ³⁰ And great crowds came to him, bringing with them the lame, the blind, the crippled, the mute, and many others, and they put them at his feet, and he healed them, ³¹ so that the crowd wondered, when they saw the mute speaking, the crippled healthy, the lame walking, and the blind seeing. And they glorified the God of Israel.

Jesus Feeds the Four Thousand

³² Then Jesus called his disciples to him and said, "I have compassion on the crowd because they have been with me now three days and have nothing to eat. And I am unwilling to send them away hungry, lest they faint on the way." ³³ And the disciples said to him, "Where are we to get enough bread in such a desolate place to feed so great a crowd?" ³⁴ And Jesus said

to them, "How many loaves do you have?" They said, "Seven, and a few small fish." ³⁵ And directing the crowd to sit down on the ground, ³⁶ he took the seven loaves and the fish, and having given thanks he broke them and gave them to the disciples, and the disciples gave them to the crowds. ³⁷ And they all ate and were satisfied. And they took up seven baskets full of the broken pieces left over. ³⁸ Those who ate were four thousand men, besides women and children. ³⁹ And after sending away the crowds, he got into the boat and went to the region of Magadan.

The Pharisees and Sadducees Demand Signs

16 And the Pharisees and Sadducees came, and to test him they asked him to show them a sign from heaven. ² He answered them, "When it is evening, you say, 'It will be fair weather, for the sky is red.' ³ And in the morning, 'It will be stormy today, for the sky is red and threatening.' You know how to interpret the appearance of the sky, but you cannot interpret the signs of the times. ⁴ An evil and adulterous generation seeks for a sign, but no sign will be given to it except the sign of Jonah." So he left them and departed.

The Leaven of the Pharisees and Sadducees

⁵ When the disciples reached the other side, they had forgotten to bring any bread. ⁶ Jesus said to them, "Watch and beware of the leaven of the Pharisees and Sadducees." ⁷ And they began discussing it among themselves, saying, "We brought no bread." ⁸ But Jesus, aware of this, said, "O you of little faith, why are you discussing among yourselves the fact that you have no bread? ⁹ Do you not yet perceive? Do you not remember the

five loaves for the five thousand, and how many baskets you gathered? [10] Or the seven loaves for the four thousand, and how many baskets you gathered? [11] How is it that you fail to understand that I did not speak about bread? Beware of the leaven of the Pharisees and Sadducees." [12] Then they understood that he did not tell them to beware of the leaven of bread, but of the teaching of the Pharisees and Sadducees.

Peter Confesses Jesus as the Christ

[13] Now when Jesus came into the district of Caesarea Philippi, he asked his disciples, "Who do people say that the Son of Man is?" [14] And they said, "Some say John the Baptist, others say Elijah, and others Jeremiah or one of the prophets." [15] He said to them, "But who do you say that I am?" [16] Simon Peter replied, "You are the Christ, the Son of the living God." [17] And Jesus answered him, "Blessed are you, Simon Bar-Jonah! For flesh and blood has not revealed this to you, but my Father who is in heaven. [18] And I tell you, you are Peter, and on this rock I will build my church, and the gates of hell shall not prevail against it. [19] I will give you the keys of the kingdom of heaven, and whatever you bind on earth shall be bound in heaven, and whatever you loose on earth shall be loosed in heaven." [20] Then he strictly charged the disciples to tell no one that he was the Christ.

Jesus Foretells His Death and Resurrection

[21] From that time Jesus began to show his disciples that he must go to Jerusalem and suffer many things from the elders and chief priests and scribes, and be killed, and on the third day be raised. [22] And Peter took him aside and began to rebuke him,

saying, "Far be it from you, Lord! This shall never happen to you." **23** But he turned and said to Peter, "Get behind me, Satan! You are a hindrance to me. For you are not setting your mind on the things of God, but on the things of man."

Take Up Your Cross and Follow Jesus

24 Then Jesus told his disciples, "If anyone would come after me, let him deny himself and take up his cross and follow me. **25** For whoever would save his life will lose it, but whoever loses his life for my sake will find it. **26** For what will it profit a man if he gains the whole world and forfeits his soul? Or what shall a man give in return for his soul? **27** For the Son of Man is going to come with his angels in the glory of his Father, and then he will repay each person according to what he has done. **28** Truly, I say to you, there are some standing here who will not taste death until they see the Son of Man coming in his kingdom."

The Transfiguration

17 And after six days Jesus took with him Peter and James, and John his brother, and led them up a high mountain by themselves. **2** And he was transfigured before them, and his face shone like the sun, and his clothes became white as light. **3** And behold, there appeared to them Moses and Elijah, talking with him. **4** And Peter said to Jesus, "Lord, it is good that we are here. If you wish, I will make three tents here, one for you and one for Moses and one for Elijah." **5** He was still speaking when, behold, a bright cloud overshadowed them, and a voice from the cloud said, "This is my beloved Son, with whom I am well pleased; listen to him." **6** When the disciples heard this, they fell

on their faces and were terrified. ⁷ But Jesus came and touched them, saying, "Rise, and have no fear." ⁸ And when they lifted up their eyes, they saw no one but Jesus only.

⁹ And as they were coming down the mountain, Jesus commanded them, "Tell no one the vision, until the Son of Man is raised from the dead." ¹⁰ And the disciples asked him, "Then why do the scribes say that first Elijah must come?" ¹¹ He answered, "Elijah does come, and he will restore all things. ¹² But I tell you that Elijah has already come, and they did not recognize him, but did to him whatever they pleased. So also the Son of Man will certainly suffer at their hands." ¹³ Then the disciples understood that he was speaking to them of John the Baptist.

Jesus Heals a Boy with a Demon

¹⁴ And when they came to the crowd, a man came up to him and, kneeling before him, ¹⁵ said, "Lord, have mercy on my son, for he has seizures and he suffers terribly. For often he falls into the fire, and often into the water. ¹⁶ And I brought him to your disciples, and they could not heal him." ¹⁷ And Jesus answered, "O faithless and twisted generation, how long am I to be with you? How long am I to bear with you? Bring him here to me." ¹⁸ And Jesus rebuked the demon, and it came out of him, and the boy was healed instantly. ¹⁹ Then the disciples came to Jesus privately and said, "Why could we not cast it out?" ²⁰ He said to them, "Because of your little faith. For truly, I say to you, if you have faith like a grain of mustard seed, you will say to this mountain, 'Move from here to there,' and it will move, and nothing will be impossible for you."

Jesus Again Foretells Death, Resurrection

²² As they were gathering in Galilee, Jesus said to them, "The Son of Man is about to be delivered into the hands of men, ²³ and they will kill him, and he will be raised on the third day." And they were greatly distressed.

The Temple Tax

²⁴ When they came to Capernaum, the collectors of the two-drachma tax went up to Peter and said, "Does your teacher not pay the tax?" ²⁵ He said, "Yes." And when he came into the house, Jesus spoke to him first, saying, "What do you think, Simon? From whom do kings of the earth take toll or tax? From their sons or from others?" ²⁶ And when he said, "From others," Jesus said to him, "Then the sons are free. ²⁷ However, not to give offense to them, go to the sea and cast a hook and take the first fish that comes up, and when you open its mouth you will find a shekel. Take that and give it to them for me and for yourself."

Who Is the Greatest?

18 At that time the disciples came to Jesus, saying, "Who is the greatest in the kingdom of heaven?" ² And calling to him a child, he put him in the midst of them ³ and said, "Truly, I say to you, unless you turn and become like children, you will never enter the kingdom of heaven. ⁴ Whoever humbles himself like this child is the greatest in the kingdom of heaven.

⁵ "Whoever receives one such child in my name receives me, ⁶ but whoever causes one of these little ones who believe in me to sin, it would be better for him to have a great millstone fastened around his neck and to be drowned in the depth of the sea.

Temptations to Sin

⁷ "Woe to the world for temptations to sin! For it is necessary that temptations come, but woe to the one by whom the temptation comes! ⁸ And if your hand or your foot causes you to sin, cut it off and throw it away. It is better for you to enter life crippled or lame than with two hands or two feet to be thrown into the eternal fire. ⁹ And if your eye causes you to sin, tear it out and throw it away. It is better for you to enter life with one eye than with two eyes to be thrown into the hell of fire.

The Parable of the Lost Sheep

¹⁰ "See that you do not despise one of these little ones. For I tell you that in heaven their angels always see the face of my Father who is in heaven. ¹² What do you think? If a man has a hundred sheep, and one of them has gone astray, does he not leave the ninety-nine on the mountains and go in search of the one that went astray? ¹³ And if he finds it, truly, I say to you, he rejoices over it more than over the ninety-nine that never went astray. ¹⁴ So it is not the will of my Father who is in heaven that one of these little ones should perish.

If Your Brother Sins Against You

¹⁵ "If your brother sins against you, go and tell him his fault, between you and him alone. If he listens to you, you have gained your brother. ¹⁶ But if he does not listen, take one or two others along with you, that every charge may be established by the evidence of two or three witnesses. ¹⁷ If he refuses to listen to them, tell it to the church. And if he refuses to listen even to the church, let him be to you as a Gentile and a tax collector. ¹⁸ Truly, I say to you, whatever you bind on earth shall be bound

in heaven, and whatever you loose on earth shall be loosed in heaven. [19] Again I say to you, if two of you agree on earth about anything they ask, it will be done for them by my Father in heaven. [20] For where two or three are gathered in my name, there am I among them."

The Parable of the Unforgiving Servant

[21] Then Peter came up and said to him, "Lord, how often will my brother sin against me, and I forgive him? As many as seven times?" [22] Jesus said to him, "I do not say to you seven times, but seventy-seven times.

[23] "Therefore the kingdom of heaven may be compared to a king who wished to settle accounts with his servants. [24] When he began to settle, one was brought to him who owed him ten thousand talents. [25] And since he could not pay, his master ordered him to be sold, with his wife and children and all that he had, and payment to be made. [26] So the servant fell on his knees, imploring him, 'Have patience with me, and I will pay you everything.' [27] And out of pity for him, the master of that servant released him and forgave him the debt. [28] But when that same servant went out, he found one of his fellow servants who owed him a hundred denarii, and seizing him, he began to choke him, saying, 'Pay what you owe.' [29] So his fellow servant fell down and pleaded with him, 'Have patience with me, and I will pay you.' [30] He refused and went and put him in prison until he should pay the debt. [31] When his fellow servants saw what had taken place, they were greatly distressed, and they went and reported to their master all that had taken place. [32] Then his master summoned him and said to him, 'You wicked servant! I forgave you all that debt because you pleaded

with me. ³³ And should not you have had mercy on your fellow servant, as I had mercy on you?' ³⁴ And in anger his master delivered him to the jailers, until he should pay all his debt. ³⁵ So also my heavenly Father will do to every one of you, if you do not forgive your brother from your heart."

Teaching About Divorce

19 Now when Jesus had finished these sayings, he went away from Galilee and entered the region of Judea beyond the Jordan. ² And large crowds followed him, and he healed them there.

³ And Pharisees came up to him and tested him by asking, "Is it lawful to divorce one's wife for any cause?" ⁴ He answered, "Have you not read that he who created them from the beginning made them male and female, ⁵ and said, 'Therefore a man shall leave his father and his mother and hold fast to his wife, and the two shall become one flesh'? ⁶ So they are no longer two but one flesh. What therefore God has joined together, let not man separate." ⁷ They said to him, "Why then did Moses command one to give a certificate of divorce and to send her away?" ⁸ He said to them, "Because of your hardness of heart Moses allowed you to divorce your wives, but from the beginning it was not so. ⁹ And I say to you: whoever divorces his wife, except for sexual immorality, and marries another, commits adultery."

¹⁰ The disciples said to him, "If such is the case of a man with his wife, it is better not to marry." ¹¹ But he said to them, "Not everyone can receive this saying, but only those to whom it is given. ¹² For there are eunuchs who have been so from birth, and there are eunuchs who have been made eunuchs by men, and there are eunuchs who have made themselves eunuchs for

the sake of the kingdom of heaven. Let the one who is able to receive this receive it."

Let the Children Come to Me

¹³ Then children were brought to him that he might lay his hands on them and pray. The disciples rebuked the people, ¹⁴ but Jesus said, "Let the little children come to me and do not hinder them, for to such belongs the kingdom of heaven." ¹⁵ And he laid his hands on them and went away.

The Rich Young Man

¹⁶ And behold, a man came up to him, saying, "Teacher, what good deed must I do to have eternal life?" ¹⁷ And he said to him, "Why do you ask me about what is good? There is only one who is good. If you would enter life, keep the commandments." ¹⁸ He said to him, "Which ones?" And Jesus said, "You shall not murder, You shall not commit adultery, You shall not steal, You shall not bear false witness, ¹⁹ Honor your father and mother, and, You shall love your neighbor as yourself." ²⁰ The young man said to him, "All these I have kept. What do I still lack?" ²¹ Jesus said to him, "If you would be perfect, go, sell what you possess and give to the poor, and you will have treasure in heaven; and come, follow me." ²² When the young man heard this he went away sorrowful, for he had great possessions.

²³ And Jesus said to his disciples, "Truly, I say to you, only with difficulty will a rich person enter the kingdom of heaven. ²⁴ Again I tell you, it is easier for a camel to go through the eye of a needle than for a rich person to enter the kingdom of God." ²⁵ When the disciples heard this, they were greatly astonished, saying, "Who then can be saved?" ²⁶ But Jesus looked at them

and said, "With man this is impossible, but with God all things are possible." **27** Then Peter said in reply, "See, we have left everything and followed you. What then will we have?" **28** Jesus said to them, "Truly, I say to you, in the new world, when the Son of Man will sit on his glorious throne, you who have followed me will also sit on twelve thrones, judging the twelve tribes of Israel. **29** And everyone who has left houses or brothers or sisters or father or mother or children or lands, for my name's sake, will receive a hundredfold and will inherit eternal life. **30** But many who are first will be last, and the last first.

Laborers in the Vineyard

20 "For the kingdom of heaven is like a master of a house who went out early in the morning to hire laborers for his vineyard. **2** After agreeing with the laborers for a denarius a day, he sent them into his vineyard. **3** And going out about the third hour he saw others standing idle in the marketplace, **4** and to them he said, 'You go into the vineyard too, and whatever is right I will give you.' **5** So they went. Going out again about the sixth hour and the ninth hour, he did the same. **6** And about the eleventh hour he went out and found others standing. And he said to them, 'Why do you stand here idle all day?' **7** They said to him, 'Because no one has hired us.' He said to them, 'You go into the vineyard too.' **8** And when evening came, the owner of the vineyard said to his foreman, 'Call the laborers and pay them their wages, beginning with the last, up to the first.' **9** And when those hired about the eleventh hour came, each of them received a denarius. **10** Now when those hired first came, they thought they would receive more, but each of them also received a denarius. **11** And on receiving it they grumbled at

the master of the house, ¹² saying, 'These last worked only one hour, and you have made them equal to us who have borne the burden of the day and the scorching heat.' ¹³ But he replied to one of them, 'Friend, I am doing you no wrong. Did you not agree with me for a denarius? ¹⁴ Take what belongs to you and go. I choose to give to this last worker as I give to you. ¹⁵ Am I not allowed to do what I choose with what belongs to me? Or do you begrudge my generosity?' ¹⁶ So the last will be first, and the first last."

Jesus Foretells His Death a Third Time

¹⁷ And as Jesus was going up to Jerusalem, he took the twelve disciples aside, and on the way he said to them, ¹⁸ "See, we are going up to Jerusalem. And the Son of Man will be delivered over to the chief priests and scribes, and they will condemn him to death ¹⁹ and deliver him over to the Gentiles to be mocked and flogged and crucified, and he will be raised on the third day."

A Mother's Request

²⁰ Then the mother of the sons of Zebedee came up to him with her sons, and kneeling before him she asked him for something. ²¹ And he said to her, "What do you want?" She said to him, "Say that these two sons of mine are to sit, one at your right hand and one at your left, in your kingdom." ²² Jesus answered, "You do not know what you are asking. Are you able to drink the cup that I am to drink?" They said to him, "We are able." ²³ He said to them, "You will drink my cup, but to sit at my right hand and at my left is not mine to grant, but it is for those for whom it has been prepared by my Father." ²⁴ And

when the ten heard it, they were indignant at the two brothers. ²⁵ But Jesus called them to him and said, "You know that the rulers of the Gentiles lord it over them, and their great ones exercise authority over them. ²⁶ It shall not be so among you. But whoever would be great among you must be your servant, ²⁷ and whoever would be first among you must be your slave, ²⁸ even as the Son of Man came not to be served but to serve, and to give his life as a ransom for many."

Jesus Heals Two Blind Men

²⁹ And as they went out of Jericho, a great crowd followed him. ³⁰ And behold, there were two blind men sitting by the roadside, and when they heard that Jesus was passing by, they cried out, "Lord, have mercy on us, Son of David!" ³¹ The crowd rebuked them, telling them to be silent, but they cried out all the more, "Lord, have mercy on us, Son of David!" ³² And stopping, Jesus called them and said, "What do you want me to do for you?" ³³ They said to him, "Lord, let our eyes be opened." ³⁴ And Jesus in pity touched their eyes, and immediately they recovered their sight and followed him.

The Triumphal Entry

21 Now when they drew near to Jerusalem and came to Bethphage, to the Mount of Olives, then Jesus sent two disciples, ² saying to them, "Go into the village in front of you, and immediately you will find a donkey tied, and a colt with her. Untie them and bring them to me. ³ If anyone says anything to you, you shall say, 'The Lord needs them,' and he will send them at once." ⁴ This took place to fulfill what was spoken by the prophet, saying,

⁵   "Say to the daughter of Zion,
       'Behold, your king is coming to you,
            humble, and mounted on a donkey,
            on a colt, the foal of a beast of burden.'"

⁶ The disciples went and did as Jesus had directed them.
⁷ They brought the donkey and the colt and put on them their
cloaks, and he sat on them. ⁸ Most of the crowd spread their
cloaks on the road, and others cut branches from the trees
and spread them on the road. ⁹ And the crowds that went
before him and that followed him were shouting, "Hosanna
to the Son of David! Blessed is he who comes in the name of
the Lord! Hosanna in the highest!" ¹⁰ And when he entered
Jerusalem, the whole city was stirred up, saying, "Who is
this?" ¹¹ And the crowds said, "This is the prophet Jesus, from
Nazareth of Galilee."

Jesus Cleanses the Temple

¹² And Jesus entered the temple and drove out all who sold
and bought in the temple, and he overturned the tables of
the money-changers and the seats of those who sold pigeons.
¹³ He said to them, "It is written, 'My house shall be called a
house of prayer,' but you make it a den of robbers."

¹⁴ And the blind and the lame came to him in the temple,
and he healed them. ¹⁵ But when the chief priests and the
scribes saw the wonderful things that he did, and the children crying out in the temple, "Hosanna to the Son of David!"
they were indignant, ¹⁶ and they said to him, "Do you hear
what these are saying?" And Jesus said to them, "Yes; have you
never read,

"'Out of the mouth of infants and nursing babies
you have prepared praise'?"

¹⁷ And leaving them, he went out of the city to Bethany and
lodged there.

Jesus Curses the Fig Tree

¹⁸ In the morning, as he was returning to the city, he
became hungry. ¹⁹ And seeing a fig tree by the wayside, he went
to it and found nothing on it but only leaves. And he said to
it, "May no fruit ever come from you again!" And the fig tree
withered at once.

²⁰ When the disciples saw it, they marveled, saying, "How
did the fig tree wither at once?" ²¹ And Jesus answered them,
"Truly, I say to you, if you have faith and do not doubt, you will
not only do what has been done to the fig tree, but even if you
say to this mountain, 'Be taken up and thrown into the sea,' it
will happen. ²² And whatever you ask in prayer, you will receive,
if you have faith."

The Authority of Jesus Challenged

²³ And when he entered the temple, the chief priests and the
elders of the people came up to him as he was teaching, and
said, "By what authority are you doing these things, and who
gave you this authority?" ²⁴ Jesus answered them, "I also will
ask you one question, and if you tell me the answer, then I also
will tell you by what authority I do these things. ²⁵ The baptism
of John, from where did it come? From heaven or from man?"
And they discussed it among themselves, saying, "If we say,
'From heaven,' he will say to us, 'Why then did you not believe

him?' ²⁶ But if we say, 'From man,' we are afraid of the crowd, for they all hold that John was a prophet." ²⁷ So they answered Jesus, "We do not know." And he said to them, "Neither will I tell you by what authority I do these things.

The Parable of the Two Sons

²⁸ "What do you think? A man had two sons. And he went to the first and said, 'Son, go and work in the vineyard today.' ²⁹ And he answered, 'I will not,' but afterward he changed his mind and went. ³⁰ And he went to the other son and said the same. And he answered, 'I go, sir,' but did not go. ³¹ Which of the two did the will of his father?" They said, "The first." Jesus said to them, "Truly, I say to you, the tax collectors and the prostitutes go into the kingdom of God before you. ³² For John came to you in the way of righteousness, and you did not believe him, but the tax collectors and the prostitutes believed him. And even when you saw it, you did not afterward change your minds and believe him.

The Parable of the Tenants

³³ "Hear another parable. There was a master of a house who planted a vineyard and put a fence around it and dug a winepress in it and built a tower and leased it to tenants, and went into another country. ³⁴ When the season for fruit drew near, he sent his servants to the tenants to get his fruit. ³⁵ And the tenants took his servants and beat one, killed another, and stoned another. ³⁶ Again he sent other servants, more than the first. And they did the same to them. ³⁷ Finally he sent his son to them, saying, 'They will respect my son.' ³⁸ But when the tenants saw the son, they said to themselves, 'This is the heir.

Come, let us kill him and have his inheritance.' ³⁹ And they took him and threw him out of the vineyard and killed him. ⁴⁰ When therefore the owner of the vineyard comes, what will he do to those tenants?" ⁴¹ They said to him, "He will put those wretches to a miserable death and let out the vineyard to other tenants who will give him the fruits in their seasons."

⁴² Jesus said to them, "Have you never read in the Scriptures:

> " 'The stone that the builders rejected
>   has become the cornerstone;
>   this was the Lord's doing,
>   and it is marvelous in our eyes'?

⁴³ Therefore I tell you, the kingdom of God will be taken away from you and given to a people producing its fruits. ⁴⁴ And the one who falls on this stone will be broken to pieces; and when it falls on anyone, it will crush him."

⁴⁵ When the chief priests and the Pharisees heard his parables, they perceived that he was speaking about them. ⁴⁶ And although they were seeking to arrest him, they feared the crowds, because they held him to be a prophet.

The Parable of the Wedding Feast

22 And again Jesus spoke to them in parables, saying, ² "The kingdom of heaven may be compared to a king who gave a wedding feast for his son, ³ and sent his servants to call those who were invited to the wedding feast, but they would not come. ⁴ Again he sent other servants, saying, 'Tell those who are invited, "See, I have prepared my dinner, my oxen and my fat calves have been slaughtered, and everything is ready. Come

to the wedding feast."' ⁵ But they paid no attention and went off, one to his farm, another to his business, ⁶ while the rest seized his servants, treated them shamefully, and killed them. ⁷ The king was angry, and he sent his troops and destroyed those murderers and burned their city. ⁸ Then he said to his servants, 'The wedding feast is ready, but those invited were not worthy. ⁹ Go therefore to the main roads and invite to the wedding feast as many as you find.' ¹⁰ And those servants went out into the roads and gathered all whom they found, both bad and good. So the wedding hall was filled with guests.

¹¹ "But when the king came in to look at the guests, he saw there a man who had no wedding garment. ¹² And he said to him, 'Friend, how did you get in here without a wedding garment?' And he was speechless. ¹³ Then the king said to the attendants, 'Bind him hand and foot and cast him into the outer darkness. In that place there will be weeping and gnashing of teeth.' ¹⁴ For many are called, but few are chosen."

Paying Taxes to Caesar

¹⁵ Then the Pharisees went and plotted how to entangle him in his words. ¹⁶ And they sent their disciples to him, along with the Herodians, saying, "Teacher, we know that you are true and teach the way of God truthfully, and you do not care about anyone's opinion, for you are not swayed by appearances. ¹⁷ Tell us, then, what you think. Is it lawful to pay taxes to Caesar, or not?" ¹⁸ But Jesus, aware of their malice, said, "Why put me to the test, you hypocrites? ¹⁹ Show me the coin for the tax." And they brought him a denarius. ²⁰ And Jesus said to them, "Whose likeness and inscription is this?" ²¹ They said, "Caesar's." Then he said to them, "Therefore render to Caesar the things that are

Caesar's, and to God the things that are God's." [22] When they heard it, they marveled. And they left him and went away.

Sadducees Ask About the Resurrection

[23] The same day Sadducees came to him, who say that there is no resurrection, and they asked him a question, [24] saying, "Teacher, Moses said, 'If a man dies having no children, his brother must marry the widow and raise up offspring for his brother.' [25] Now there were seven brothers among us. The first married and died, and having no offspring left his wife to his brother. [26] So too the second and third, down to the seventh. [27] After them all, the woman died. [28] In the resurrection, therefore, of the seven, whose wife will she be? For they all had her."

[29] But Jesus answered them, "You are wrong, because you know neither the Scriptures nor the power of God. [30] For in the resurrection they neither marry nor are given in marriage, but are like angels in heaven. [31] And as for the resurrection of the dead, have you not read what was said to you by God: [32] 'I am the God of Abraham, and the God of Isaac, and the God of Jacob'? He is not God of the dead, but of the living." [33] And when the crowd heard it, they were astonished at his teaching.

The Great Commandment

[34] But when the Pharisees heard that he had silenced the Sadducees, they gathered together. [35] And one of them, a lawyer, asked him a question to test him. [36] "Teacher, which is the great commandment in the Law?" [37] And he said to him, "You shall love the Lord your God with all your heart and with all your soul and with all your mind. [38] This is the great and first commandment. [39] And a second is like it: You shall love your

neighbor as yourself. ⁴⁰ On these two commandments depend all the Law and the Prophets."

Whose Son Is the Christ?

⁴¹ Now while the Pharisees were gathered together, Jesus asked them a question, ⁴² saying, "What do you think about the Christ? Whose son is he?" They said to him, "The son of David." ⁴³ He said to them, "How is it then that David, in the Spirit, calls him Lord, saying,

⁴⁴   " 'The Lord said to my Lord,
        "Sit at my right hand,
            until I put your enemies under your feet" '?

⁴⁵ If then David calls him Lord, how is he his son?" ⁴⁶ And no one was able to answer him a word, nor from that day did anyone dare to ask him any more questions.

Seven Woes to the Scribes and Pharisees

23 Then Jesus said to the crowds and to his disciples, ² "The scribes and the Pharisees sit on Moses' seat, ³ so do and observe whatever they tell you, but not the works they do. For they preach, but do not practice. ⁴ They tie up heavy burdens, hard to bear, and lay them on people's shoulders, but they themselves are not willing to move them with their finger. ⁵ They do all their deeds to be seen by others. For they make their phylacteries broad and their fringes long, ⁶ and they love the place of honor at feasts and the best seats in the synagogues ⁷ and greetings in the marketplaces and being called rabbi by others. ⁸ But you are not to be called rabbi, for you

have one teacher, and you are all brothers. [9] And call no man your father on earth, for you have one Father, who is in heaven. [10] Neither be called instructors, for you have one instructor, the Christ. [11] The greatest among you shall be your servant. [12] Whoever exalts himself will be humbled, and whoever humbles himself will be exalted.

[13] "But woe to you, scribes and Pharisees, hypocrites! For you shut the kingdom of heaven in people's faces. For you neither enter yourselves nor allow those who would enter to go in. [15] Woe to you, scribes and Pharisees, hypocrites! For you travel across sea and land to make a single proselyte, and when he becomes a proselyte, you make him twice as much a child of hell as yourselves.

[16] "Woe to you, blind guides, who say, 'If anyone swears by the temple, it is nothing, but if anyone swears by the gold of the temple, he is bound by his oath.' [17] You blind fools! For which is greater, the gold or the temple that has made the gold sacred? [18] And you say, 'If anyone swears by the altar, it is nothing, but if anyone swears by the gift that is on the altar, he is bound by his oath.' [19] You blind men! For which is greater, the gift or the altar that makes the gift sacred? [20] So whoever swears by the altar swears by it and by everything on it. [21] And whoever swears by the temple swears by it and by him who dwells in it. [22] And whoever swears by heaven swears by the throne of God and by him who sits upon it.

[23] "Woe to you, scribes and Pharisees, hypocrites! For you tithe mint and dill and cumin, and have neglected the weightier matters of the law: justice and mercy and faithfulness. These you ought to have done, without neglecting the others. [24] You blind guides, straining out a gnat and swallowing a camel!

[25] "Woe to you, scribes and Pharisees, hypocrites! For you clean the outside of the cup and the plate, but inside they are full of greed and self-indulgence. [26] You blind Pharisee! First clean the inside of the cup and the plate, that the outside also may be clean.

[27] "Woe to you, scribes and Pharisees, hypocrites! For you are like whitewashed tombs, which outwardly appear beautiful, but within are full of dead people's bones and all uncleanness. [28] So you also outwardly appear righteous to others, but within you are full of hypocrisy and lawlessness.

[29] "Woe to you, scribes and Pharisees, hypocrites! For you build the tombs of the prophets and decorate the monuments of the righteous, [30] saying, 'If we had lived in the days of our fathers, we would not have taken part with them in shedding the blood of the prophets.' [31] Thus you witness against yourselves that you are sons of those who murdered the prophets. [32] Fill up, then, the measure of your fathers. [33] You serpents, you brood of vipers, how are you to escape being sentenced to hell? [34] Therefore I send you prophets and wise men and scribes, some of whom you will kill and crucify, and some you will flog in your synagogues and persecute from town to town, [35] so that on you may come all the righteous blood shed on earth, from the blood of righteous Abel to the blood of Zechariah the son of Barachiah, whom you murdered between the sanctuary and the altar. [36] Truly, I say to you, all these things will come upon this generation.

Lament over Jerusalem

[37] "O Jerusalem, Jerusalem, the city that kills the prophets and stones those who are sent to it! How often would I have

gathered your children together as a hen gathers her brood under her wings, and you were not willing! ³⁸ See, your house is left to you desolate. ³⁹ For I tell you, you will not see me again, until you say, 'Blessed is he who comes in the name of the Lord.'"

Jesus Foretells Destruction of the Temple

24 Jesus left the temple and was going away, when his disciples came to point out to him the buildings of the temple. ² But he answered them, "You see all these, do you not? Truly, I say to you, there will not be left here one stone upon another that will not be thrown down."

Signs of the End of the Age

³ As he sat on the Mount of Olives, the disciples came to him privately, saying, "Tell us, when will these things be, and what will be the sign of your coming and of the end of the age?" ⁴ And Jesus answered them, "See that no one leads you astray. ⁵ For many will come in my name, saying, 'I am the Christ,' and they will lead many astray. ⁶ And you will hear of wars and rumors of wars. See that you are not alarmed, for this must take place, but the end is not yet. ⁷ For nation will rise against nation, and kingdom against kingdom, and there will be famines and earthquakes in various places. ⁸ All these are but the beginning of the birth pains.

⁹ "Then they will deliver you up to tribulation and put you to death, and you will be hated by all nations for my name's sake. ¹⁰ And then many will fall away and betray one another and hate one another. ¹¹ And many false prophets will arise and lead many astray. ¹² And because lawlessness will be increased, the love of many will grow cold. ¹³ But the one who endures to

the end will be saved. [14] And this gospel of the kingdom will be proclaimed throughout the whole world as a testimony to all nations, and then the end will come.

The Abomination of Desolation

[15] "So when you see the abomination of desolation spoken of by the prophet Daniel, standing in the holy place (let the reader understand), [16] then let those who are in Judea flee to the mountains. [17] Let the one who is on the housetop not go down to take what is in his house, [18] and let the one who is in the field not turn back to take his cloak. [19] And alas for women who are pregnant and for those who are nursing infants in those days! [20] Pray that your flight may not be in winter or on a Sabbath. [21] For then there will be great tribulation, such as has not been from the beginning of the world until now, no, and never will be. [22] And if those days had not been cut short, no human being would be saved. But for the sake of the elect those days will be cut short. [23] Then if anyone says to you, 'Look, here is the Christ!' or 'There he is!' do not believe it. [24] For false christs and false prophets will arise and perform great signs and wonders, so as to lead astray, if possible, even the elect. [25] See, I have told you beforehand. [26] So, if they say to you, 'Look, he is in the wilderness,' do not go out. If they say, 'Look, he is in the inner rooms,' do not believe it. [27] For as the lightning comes from the east and shines as far as the west, so will be the coming of the Son of Man. [28] Wherever the corpse is, there the vultures will gather.

The Coming of the Son of Man

[29] "Immediately after the tribulation of those days the sun will be darkened, and the moon will not give its light, and the

stars will fall from heaven, and the powers of the heavens will
be shaken. ³⁰ Then will appear in heaven the sign of the Son of
Man, and then all the tribes of the earth will mourn, and they
will see the Son of Man coming on the clouds of heaven with
power and great glory. ³¹ And he will send out his angels with a
loud trumpet call, and they will gather his elect from the four
winds, from one end of heaven to the other.

The Lesson of the Fig Tree

³² "From the fig tree learn its lesson: as soon as its branch
becomes tender and puts out its leaves, you know that summer
is near. ³³ So also, when you see all these things, you know that
he is near, at the very gates. ³⁴ Truly, I say to you, this generation
will not pass away until all these things take place. ³⁵ Heaven
and earth will pass away, but my words will not pass away.

No One Knows That Day and Hour

³⁶ "But concerning that day and hour no one knows, not
even the angels of heaven, nor the Son, but the Father only.
³⁷ For as were the days of Noah, so will be the coming of the Son
of Man. ³⁸ For as in those days before the flood they were eating
and drinking, marrying and giving in marriage, until the day
when Noah entered the ark, ³⁹ and they were unaware until the
flood came and swept them all away, so will be the coming of
the Son of Man. ⁴⁰ Then two men will be in the field; one will be
taken and one left. ⁴¹ Two women will be grinding at the mill;
one will be taken and one left. ⁴² Therefore, stay awake, for you
do not know on what day your Lord is coming. ⁴³ But know this,
that if the master of the house had known in what part of the
night the thief was coming, he would have stayed awake and

would not have let his house be broken into. ⁴⁴ Therefore you also must be ready, for the Son of Man is coming at an hour you do not expect.

⁴⁵ "Who then is the faithful and wise servant, whom his master has set over his household, to give them their food at the proper time? ⁴⁶ Blessed is that servant whom his master will find so doing when he comes. ⁴⁷ Truly, I say to you, he will set him over all his possessions. ⁴⁸ But if that wicked servant says to himself, 'My master is delayed,' ⁴⁹ and begins to beat his fellow servants and eats and drinks with drunkards, ⁵⁰ the master of that servant will come on a day when he does not expect him and at an hour he does not know ⁵¹ and will cut him in pieces and put him with the hypocrites. In that place there will be weeping and gnashing of teeth.

The Parable of the Ten Virgins

25 "Then the kingdom of heaven will be like ten virgins who took their lamps and went to meet the bridegroom. ² Five of them were foolish, and five were wise. ³ For when the foolish took their lamps, they took no oil with them, ⁴ but the wise took flasks of oil with their lamps. ⁵ As the bridegroom was delayed, they all became drowsy and slept. ⁶ But at midnight there was a cry, 'Here is the bridegroom! Come out to meet him.' ⁷ Then all those virgins rose and trimmed their lamps. ⁸ And the foolish said to the wise, 'Give us some of your oil, for our lamps are going out.' ⁹ But the wise answered, saying, 'Since there will not be enough for us and for you, go rather to the dealers and buy for yourselves.' ¹⁰ And while they were going to buy, the bridegroom came, and those who were ready went in with him to the marriage feast, and the door was

shut. **11** Afterward the other virgins came also, saying, 'Lord, lord, open to us.' **12** But he answered, 'Truly, I say to you, I do not know you.' **13** Watch therefore, for you know neither the day nor the hour.

The Parable of the Talents

14 "For it will be like a man going on a journey, who called his servants and entrusted to them his property. **15** To one he gave five talents, to another two, to another one, to each according to his ability. Then he went away. **16** He who had received the five talents went at once and traded with them, and he made five talents more. **17** So also he who had the two talents made two talents more. **18** But he who had received the one talent went and dug in the ground and hid his master's money. **19** Now after a long time the master of those servants came and settled accounts with them. **20** And he who had received the five talents came forward, bringing five talents more, saying, 'Master, you delivered to me five talents; here, I have made five talents more.' **21** His master said to him, 'Well done, good and faithful servant. You have been faithful over a little; I will set you over much. Enter into the joy of your master.' **22** And he also who had the two talents came forward, saying, 'Master, you delivered to me two talents; here, I have made two talents more.' **23** His master said to him, 'Well done, good and faithful servant. You have been faithful over a little; I will set you over much. Enter into the joy of your master.' **24** He also who had received the one talent came forward, saying, 'Master, I knew you to be a hard man, reaping where you did not sow, and gathering where you scattered no seed, **25** so I was afraid, and I went and hid your talent in the ground. Here, you have what is yours.' **26** But his master

answered him, 'You wicked and slothful servant! You knew that I reap where I have not sown and gather where I scattered no seed? ²⁷ Then you ought to have invested my money with the bankers, and at my coming I should have received what was my own with interest. ²⁸ So take the talent from him and give it to him who has the ten talents. ²⁹ For to everyone who has will more be given, and he will have an abundance. But from the one who has not, even what he has will be taken away. ³⁰ And cast the worthless servant into the outer darkness. In that place there will be weeping and gnashing of teeth.'

The Final Judgment

³¹ "When the Son of Man comes in his glory, and all the angels with him, then he will sit on his glorious throne. ³² Before him will be gathered all the nations, and he will separate people one from another as a shepherd separates the sheep from the goats. ³³ And he will place the sheep on his right, but the goats on the left. ³⁴ Then the King will say to those on his right, 'Come, you who are blessed by my Father, inherit the kingdom prepared for you from the foundation of the world. ³⁵ For I was hungry and you gave me food, I was thirsty and you gave me drink, I was a stranger and you welcomed me, ³⁶ I was naked and you clothed me, I was sick and you visited me, I was in prison and you came to me.' ³⁷ Then the righteous will answer him, saying, 'Lord, when did we see you hungry and feed you, or thirsty and give you drink? ³⁸ And when did we see you a stranger and welcome you, or naked and clothe you? ³⁹ And when did we see you sick or in prison and visit you?' ⁴⁰ And the King will answer them, 'Truly, I say to you, as you did it to one of the least of these my brothers, you did it to me.'

⁴¹ "Then he will say to those on his left, 'Depart from me, you cursed, into the eternal fire prepared for the devil and his angels. ⁴² For I was hungry and you gave me no food, I was thirsty and you gave me no drink, ⁴³ I was a stranger and you did not welcome me, naked and you did not clothe me, sick and in prison and you did not visit me.' ⁴⁴ Then they also will answer, saying, 'Lord, when did we see you hungry or thirsty or a stranger or naked or sick or in prison, and did not minister to you?' ⁴⁵ Then he will answer them, saying, 'Truly, I say to you, as you did not do it to one of the least of these, you did not do it to me.' ⁴⁶ And these will go away into eternal punishment, but the righteous into eternal life."

The Plot to Kill Jesus

26 When Jesus had finished all these sayings, he said to his disciples, ² "You know that after two days the Passover is coming, and the Son of Man will be delivered up to be crucified."

³ Then the chief priests and the elders of the people gathered in the palace of the high priest, whose name was Caiaphas, ⁴ and plotted together in order to arrest Jesus by stealth and kill him. ⁵ But they said, "Not during the feast, lest there be an uproar among the people."

Jesus Anointed at Bethany

⁶ Now when Jesus was at Bethany in the house of Simon the leper, ⁷ a woman came up to him with an alabaster flask of very expensive ointment, and she poured it on his head as he reclined at table. ⁸ And when the disciples saw it, they were indignant, saying, "Why this waste? ⁹ For this could have been sold for a

MATTHEW 26:10   144

large sum and given to the poor." ¹⁰ But Jesus, aware of this, said to them, "Why do you trouble the woman? For she has done a beautiful thing to me. ¹¹ For you always have the poor with you, but you will not always have me. ¹² In pouring this ointment on my body, she has done it to prepare me for burial. ¹³ Truly, I say to you, wherever this gospel is proclaimed in the whole world, what she has done will also be told in memory of her."

Judas to Betray Jesus

¹⁴ Then one of the twelve, whose name was Judas Iscariot, went to the chief priests ¹⁵ and said, "What will you give me if I deliver him over to you?" And they paid him thirty pieces of silver. ¹⁶ And from that moment he sought an opportunity to betray him.

The Passover with the Disciples

¹⁷ Now on the first day of Unleavened Bread the disciples came to Jesus, saying, "Where will you have us prepare for you to eat the Passover?" ¹⁸ He said, "Go into the city to a certain man and say to him, 'The Teacher says, My time is at hand. I will keep the Passover at your house with my disciples.'" ¹⁹ And the disciples did as Jesus had directed them, and they prepared the Passover.

²⁰ When it was evening, he reclined at table with the twelve. ²¹ And as they were eating, he said, "Truly, I say to you, one of you will betray me." ²² And they were very sorrowful and began to say to him one after another, "Is it I, Lord?" ²³ He answered, "He who has dipped his hand in the dish with me will betray me. ²⁴ The Son of Man goes as it is written of him, but woe to that man by whom the Son of Man is betrayed! It would have

been better for that man if he had not been born." **25** Judas, who would betray him, answered, "Is it I, Rabbi?" He said to him, "You have said so."

Institution of the Lord's Supper

26 Now as they were eating, Jesus took bread, and after blessing it broke it and gave it to the disciples, and said, "Take, eat; this is my body." **27** And he took a cup, and when he had given thanks he gave it to them, saying, "Drink of it, all of you, **28** for this is my blood of the covenant, which is poured out for many for the forgiveness of sins. **29** I tell you I will not drink again of this fruit of the vine until that day when I drink it new with you in my Father's kingdom."

Jesus Foretells Peter's Denial

30 And when they had sung a hymn, they went out to the Mount of Olives. **31** Then Jesus said to them, "You will all fall away because of me this night. For it is written, 'I will strike the shepherd, and the sheep of the flock will be scattered.' **32** But after I am raised up, I will go before you to Galilee." **33** Peter answered him, "Though they all fall away because of you, I will never fall away." **34** Jesus said to him, "Truly, I tell you, this very night, before the rooster crows, you will deny me three times." **35** Peter said to him, "Even if I must die with you, I will not deny you!" And all the disciples said the same.

Jesus Prays in Gethsemane

36 Then Jesus went with them to a place called Gethsemane, and he said to his disciples, "Sit here, while I go over there and pray." **37** And taking with him Peter and the two sons of Zebedee,

he began to be sorrowful and troubled. [38] Then he said to them, "My soul is very sorrowful, even to death; remain here, and watch with me." [39] And going a little farther he fell on his face and prayed, saying, "My Father, if it be possible, let this cup pass from me; nevertheless, not as I will, but as you will." [40] And he came to the disciples and found them sleeping. And he said to Peter, "So, could you not watch with me one hour? [41] Watch and pray that you may not enter into temptation. The spirit indeed is willing, but the flesh is weak." [42] Again, for the second time, he went away and prayed, "My Father, if this cannot pass unless I drink it, your will be done." [43] And again he came and found them sleeping, for their eyes were heavy. [44] So, leaving them again, he went away and prayed for the third time, saying the same words again. [45] Then he came to the disciples and said to them, "Sleep and take your rest later on. See, the hour is at hand, and the Son of Man is betrayed into the hands of sinners. [46] Rise, let us be going; see, my betrayer is at hand."

Betrayal and Arrest of Jesus

[47] While he was still speaking, Judas came, one of the twelve, and with him a great crowd with swords and clubs, from the chief priests and the elders of the people. [48] Now the betrayer had given them a sign, saying, "The one I will kiss is the man; seize him." [49] And he came up to Jesus at once and said, "Greetings, Rabbi!" And he kissed him. [50] Jesus said to him, "Friend, do what you came to do." Then they came up and laid hands on Jesus and seized him. [51] And behold, one of those who were with Jesus stretched out his hand and drew his sword and struck the servant of the high priest and cut off his ear. [52] Then Jesus said to him, "Put your sword back into its place. For all

who take the sword will perish by the sword. ⁵³ Do you think that I cannot appeal to my Father, and he will at once send me more than twelve legions of angels? ⁵⁴ But how then should the Scriptures be fulfilled, that it must be so?" ⁵⁵ At that hour Jesus said to the crowds, "Have you come out as against a robber, with swords and clubs to capture me? Day after day I sat in the temple teaching, and you did not seize me. ⁵⁶ But all this has taken place that the Scriptures of the prophets might be fulfilled." Then all the disciples left him and fled.

Jesus Before Caiaphas and the Council

⁵⁷ Then those who had seized Jesus led him to Caiaphas the high priest, where the scribes and the elders had gathered. ⁵⁸ And Peter was following him at a distance, as far as the courtyard of the high priest, and going inside he sat with the guards to see the end. ⁵⁹ Now the chief priests and the whole council were seeking false testimony against Jesus that they might put him to death, ⁶⁰ but they found none, though many false witnesses came forward. At last two came forward ⁶¹ and said, "This man said, 'I am able to destroy the temple of God, and to rebuild it in three days.'" ⁶² And the high priest stood up and said, "Have you no answer to make? What is it that these men testify against you?" ⁶³ But Jesus remained silent. And the high priest said to him, "I adjure you by the living God, tell us if you are the Christ, the Son of God." ⁶⁴ Jesus said to him, "You have said so. But I tell you, from now on you will see the Son of Man seated at the right hand of Power and coming on the clouds of heaven." ⁶⁵ Then the high priest tore his robes and said, "He has uttered blasphemy. What further witnesses do we need? You have now heard his blasphemy. ⁶⁶ What is your

judgment?" They answered, "He deserves death." ⁶⁷ Then they spit in his face and struck him. And some slapped him, ⁶⁸ saying, "Prophesy to us, you Christ! Who is it that struck you?"

Peter Denies Jesus

⁶⁹ Now Peter was sitting outside in the courtyard. And a servant girl came up to him and said, "You also were with Jesus the Galilean." ⁷⁰ But he denied it before them all, saying, "I do not know what you mean." ⁷¹ And when he went out to the entrance, another servant girl saw him, and she said to the bystanders, "This man was with Jesus of Nazareth." ⁷² And again he denied it with an oath: "I do not know the man." ⁷³ After a little while the bystanders came up and said to Peter, "Certainly you too are one of them, for your accent betrays you." ⁷⁴ Then he began to invoke a curse on himself and to swear, "I do not know the man." And immediately the rooster crowed. ⁷⁵ And Peter remembered the saying of Jesus, "Before the rooster crows, you will deny me three times." And he went out and wept bitterly.

Jesus Delivered to Pilate

27 When morning came, all the chief priests and the elders of the people took counsel against Jesus to put him to death. ² And they bound him and led him away and delivered him over to Pilate the governor.

Judas Hangs Himself

³ Then when Judas, his betrayer, saw that Jesus was condemned, he changed his mind and brought back the thirty pieces of silver to the chief priests and the elders, ⁴ saying,

"I have sinned by betraying innocent blood." They said, "What is that to us? See to it yourself." ⁵ And throwing down the pieces of silver into the temple, he departed, and he went and hanged himself. ⁶ But the chief priests, taking the pieces of silver, said, "It is not lawful to put them into the treasury, since it is blood money." ⁷ So they took counsel and bought with them the potter's field as a burial place for strangers. ⁸ Therefore that field has been called the Field of Blood to this day. ⁹ Then was fulfilled what had been spoken by the prophet Jeremiah, saying, "And they took the thirty pieces of silver, the price of him on whom a price had been set by some of the sons of Israel, ¹⁰ and they gave them for the potter's field, as the Lord directed me."

Jesus Before Pilate

¹¹ Now Jesus stood before the governor, and the governor asked him, "Are you the King of the Jews?" Jesus said, "You have said so." ¹² But when he was accused by the chief priests and elders, he gave no answer. ¹³ Then Pilate said to him, "Do you not hear how many things they testify against you?" ¹⁴ But he gave him no answer, not even to a single charge, so that the governor was greatly amazed.

The Crowd Chooses Barabbas

¹⁵ Now at the feast the governor was accustomed to release for the crowd any one prisoner whom they wanted. ¹⁶ And they had then a notorious prisoner called Barabbas. ¹⁷ So when they had gathered, Pilate said to them, "Whom do you want me to release for you: Barabbas, or Jesus who is called Christ?" ¹⁸ For he knew that it was out of envy that they had delivered

him up. [19] Besides, while he was sitting on the judgment seat, his wife sent word to him, "Have nothing to do with that righteous man, for I have suffered much because of him today in a dream." [20] Now the chief priests and the elders persuaded the crowd to ask for Barabbas and destroy Jesus. [21] The governor again said to them, "Which of the two do you want me to release for you?" And they said, "Barabbas." [22] Pilate said to them, "Then what shall I do with Jesus who is called Christ?" They all said, "Let him be crucified!" [23] And he said, "Why? What evil has he done?" But they shouted all the more, "Let him be crucified!"

Pilate Delivers Jesus to Be Crucified

[24] So when Pilate saw that he was gaining nothing, but rather that a riot was beginning, he took water and washed his hands before the crowd, saying, "I am innocent of this man's blood; see to it yourselves." [25] And all the people answered, "His blood be on us and on our children!" [26] Then he released for them Barabbas, and having scourged Jesus, delivered him to be crucified.

Jesus Is Mocked

[27] Then the soldiers of the governor took Jesus into the governor's headquarters, and they gathered the whole battalion before him. [28] And they stripped him and put a scarlet robe on him, [29] and twisting together a crown of thorns, they put it on his head and put a reed in his right hand. And kneeling before him, they mocked him, saying, "Hail, King of the Jews!" [30] And they spit on him and took the reed and struck him on the head. [31] And when they had mocked him, they stripped

him of the robe and put his own clothes on him and led him away to crucify him.

The Crucifixion

³²As they went out, they found a man of Cyrene, Simon by name. They compelled this man to carry his cross. ³³And when they came to a place called Golgotha (which means Place of a Skull), ³⁴they offered him wine to drink, mixed with gall, but when he tasted it, he would not drink it. ³⁵And when they had crucified him, they divided his garments among them by casting lots. ³⁶Then they sat down and kept watch over him there. ³⁷And over his head they put the charge against him, which read, "This is Jesus, the King of the Jews." ³⁸Then two robbers were crucified with him, one on the right and one on the left. ³⁹And those who passed by derided him, wagging their heads ⁴⁰and saying, "You who would destroy the temple and rebuild it in three days, save yourself! If you are the Son of God, come down from the cross." ⁴¹So also the chief priests, with the scribes and elders, mocked him, saying, ⁴²"He saved others; he cannot save himself. He is the King of Israel; let him come down now from the cross, and we will believe in him. ⁴³He trusts in God; let God deliver him now, if he desires him. For he said, 'I am the Son of God.'" ⁴⁴And the robbers who were crucified with him also reviled him in the same way.

The Death of Jesus

⁴⁵Now from the sixth hour there was darkness over all the land until the ninth hour. ⁴⁶And about the ninth hour Jesus cried out with a loud voice, saying, "Eli, Eli, lema sabachthani?" that is, "My God, my God, why have you forsaken me?" ⁴⁷And

some of the bystanders, hearing it, said, "This man is calling Elijah." [48] And one of them at once ran and took a sponge, filled it with sour wine, and put it on a reed and gave it to him to drink. [49] But the others said, "Wait, let us see whether Elijah will come to save him." [50] And Jesus cried out again with a loud voice and yielded up his spirit.

[51] And behold, the curtain of the temple was torn in two, from top to bottom. And the earth shook, and the rocks were split. [52] The tombs also were opened. And many bodies of the saints who had fallen asleep were raised, [53] and coming out of the tombs after his resurrection they went into the holy city and appeared to many. [54] When the centurion and those who were with him, keeping watch over Jesus, saw the earthquake and what took place, they were filled with awe and said, "Truly this was the Son of God!"

[55] There were also many women there, looking on from a distance, who had followed Jesus from Galilee, ministering to him, [56] among whom were Mary Magdalene and Mary the mother of James and Joseph and the mother of the sons of Zebedee.

Jesus Is Buried

[57] When it was evening, there came a rich man from Arimathea, named Joseph, who also was a disciple of Jesus. [58] He went to Pilate and asked for the body of Jesus. Then Pilate ordered it to be given to him. [59] And Joseph took the body and wrapped it in a clean linen shroud [60] and laid it in his own new tomb, which he had cut in the rock. And he rolled a great stone to the entrance of the tomb and went away. [61] Mary Magdalene and the other Mary were there, sitting opposite the tomb.

The Guard at the Tomb

[62] The next day, that is, after the day of Preparation, the chief priests and the Pharisees gathered before Pilate [63] and said, "Sir, we remember how that impostor said, while he was still alive, 'After three days I will rise.' [64] Therefore order the tomb to be made secure until the third day, lest his disciples go and steal him away and tell the people, 'He has risen from the dead,' and the last fraud will be worse than the first." [65] Pilate said to them, "You have a guard of soldiers. Go, make it as secure as you can." [66] So they went and made the tomb secure by sealing the stone and setting a guard.

The Resurrection

28 Now after the Sabbath, toward the dawn of the first day of the week, Mary Magdalene and the other Mary went to see the tomb. [2] And behold, there was a great earthquake, for an angel of the Lord descended from heaven and came and rolled back the stone and sat on it. [3] His appearance was like lightning, and his clothing white as snow. [4] And for fear of him the guards trembled and became like dead men. [5] But the angel said to the women, "Do not be afraid, for I know that you seek Jesus who was crucified. [6] He is not here, for he has risen, as he said. Come, see the place where he lay. [7] Then go quickly and tell his disciples that he has risen from the dead, and behold, he is going before you to Galilee; there you will see him. See, I have told you." [8] So they departed quickly from the tomb with fear and great joy, and ran to tell his disciples. [9] And behold, Jesus met them and said, "Greetings!" And they came up and took hold of his feet and worshiped him. [10] Then Jesus said to them, "Do not be

afraid; go and tell my brothers to go to Galilee, and there they will see me."

The Report of the Guard

¹¹ While they were going, behold, some of the guard went into the city and told the chief priests all that had taken place. ¹² And when they had assembled with the elders and taken counsel, they gave a sufficient sum of money to the soldiers ¹³ and said, "Tell people, 'His disciples came by night and stole him away while we were asleep.' ¹⁴ And if this comes to the governor's ears, we will satisfy him and keep you out of trouble." ¹⁵ So they took the money and did as they were directed. And this story has been spread among the Jews to this day.

The Great Commission

¹⁶ Now the eleven disciples went to Galilee, to the mountain to which Jesus had directed them. ¹⁷ And when they saw him they worshiped him, but some doubted. ¹⁸ And Jesus came and said to them, "All authority in heaven and on earth has been given to me. ¹⁹ Go therefore and make disciples of all nations, baptizing them in the name of the Father and of the Son and of the Holy Spirit, ²⁰ teaching them to observe all that I have commanded you. And behold, I am with you always, to the end of the age."